To my _____ Pro-Am

_____ ____ment who are

helping the Children's

Hospital ———

signature

D1238389

A
HOUSE
DIVIDED

A
HOUSE
DIVIDED

America's Strategy Gap

Melvin R. Laird

CHICAGO • 1962
HENRY REGNERY COMPANY

© *1962 Henry Regnery Company*

Manufactured in the United States of America

Library of Congress Catalog Card No. 62-20976

ACKNOWLEDGEMENTS

IN THE PREPARATION of this book I am greatly indebted to my many friends in the academic world whose original research and deep insight into the numerous problems of foreign and military policy have greatly helped to clarify my own thoughts. While too numerous to mention here, many are identified throughout the book. The members and staff of the House Defense Appropriations Subcommittee have made an almost daily contribution to my continuing education in defense matters.

For able editorial and stylistic assistance in the final stages of the book, my deep thanks are expressed to Karl Hess.

Grateful appreciation is also expressed for research and assistance to William J. Baroody, Jr. and the other members of my staff.

Without the sympathetic understanding and devoted encouragement of my wife Barbara, no effort in public life would be possible or successful.

CONTENTS

PART I

The Crisis in American Strategy

1

THE DIALOGUE

BY CHRONOLOGICAL COINCIDENCE, every one of us shares a common destiny; regardless of race, nation, or individual location we will, every one of us, die either in the latter years of the Twentieth century or in the early part of the Twenty-first. Therefore, the question of physical life is already answered for us, as it has been for each generation of man. Only details of days, months, years—or hours—are unresolved.

By political coincidence, however, this relatively brief span of mortal time involves in our era what no other age has ever confronted: the techniques of communications and conflict that make it possible to change governments and borders decisively, quickly—even explosively —without waiting for the slower processes that have marked the past. Within a single generation, today, we can make or break our world; what we do will affect not only our own lives and mode of living but also the lives and conditions of peoples in the remotest corners of the earth. Speed-up in political technology is as much a fact of our era as is the technological speed-up in modern science, where months are the span between major breakthroughs, not decades as was once the case.

This is globally significant; it also carries deep per-

3

sonal meaning. We are now, by the convergence of all the multiplying, accelerating vectors of our time, participants in a crucial *decision,* perhaps the most crucial the world has ever seen. Its outcome will be visible not alone to readers of future textbooks, but to us as the responsible participants, who by our action or inaction must determine the fate of the globe.

If we are to follow the finest portion of the heritage given us by the slow past, we will therefore above all participate consciously and actively in the decision, not being content to stand aside and watch it unfold. We will participate in terms of rational dialogue, not merely in terms of partisan passions or superficial bias. We should not, for instance, say that the pivotal issue of our crucial time is some detail of an economic system or social order—the gold standard versus nonmetallic currency, or military juntas versus parliaments. Because we have at our disposal the means to ultimate decision-making, we must look for issues of ultimate importance. We must discuss these issues in terms of real alternatives and their real consequences.

First must come the problem of life's meaning. It is a mark of the depth of our era's crisis that this dialogue is going on about us every day, from the level of international diplomacy to our own domestic conversations. It comes to the surface even in the talks we have with our children. Essentially, what is being discussed is a bracketed pair of questions—is life, biological life itself, the object most demanding of preservation? Or is the condition of life, the way people live it, the ultimate essential? Every school child knows the mode of the historical American response; the words of Patrick Henry and those like him have been echoing in our texts ever

since 1775. Life is secondary; liberty is primary. But
is primacy of values over existence still valid today?

In our present dialogue we would hear immediately
(we would be forced to by our era's situation and its
prevailing emotions) that Patrick Henry was making an
individual choice for which he could pay, individually.
Today, it is reasonably argued that the musket has been
replaced by the nuclear bomb, and decisions by national
leaders are tendered in currency which all mankind
must, willingly or unwillingly, co-sign. But in actuality
the difference between the force of massed muskets and
the horror of massed bombs is a difference only in
degree, vast and stupifying, hideous with terror, but
nevertheless not a difference in kind. And it is the
difference in kind which we can now see distinguishes
the decisions that are at the core of our history from
the existential decisions our leaders are making in
the present. Our dialogue must penetrate to the essence
of the problem: is the fact that more lives are involved
in decisions today sufficient in itself to make the condition of life secondary to the primacy of biological
preservation?

Man, even to atheists, is a thinking animal, distinguished thus from the other animals. An essential part
of his thinking has always been involved with a decision
to risk or even sacrifice life, rather than to degrade
it. In our dialogue of today, we must ask if a time has
come when man can no longer maintain the freedom of
that decision; must he now stop being a reflective animal
in order to become a reflexive animal, acting first to
preserve his life and putting aside the thought as to how
that life must subsequently be lived.

Man, to those who are not atheists, has never owed his

principal obligation to his physical life. He has owed
it, rather, to the manner of that life and its relationship
to his God. The dialogue must consider the durability
of this conviction as well. A perceptive commentary on
this question was afforded by the American theologian,
John Courtney Murray, in his recent book, *We Hold
These Truths.* In an exposition that defines the intru-
sion of the barbarian into a supposedly civilized society,
Murray said:

Society becomes barbarian when men are huddled together under the rule of force and fear; when economic
interests assume the primacy over higher values; when
material standards of mass and quantity crush out the
values of quality and excellence; . . . when the state
reaches the paradoxical point of being everywhere in-
trusive and also impotent, possessed of immense power
and powerless to achieve rational ends; when the ways
of men come under the sway of the instinctual, the
impulsive, the compulsive.

In a true dialogue problems must be discussed within
the context of mutual goodwill. As Murray also notes,
". . . barbarism threatens, when dialogue gives way to a
series of monologues; when the parties to the conversation cease to listen to one another. . . ." In rational
dialogue sober consensus is required. Who among us
would be truly responsible if he were, on the basis of
his own bias, to decide that everyone should die? He
would be a madman. Similarly, then, can we entrust to
undiscussed passion any decision claiming that, in order
to live, everyone must accept any condition of life
offered, regardless of its nature? Is that not also the
absolutism of a madman? How can one presume to
speak for all on such a matter?

As a people we have hardly begun to resolve these questions in any form even approaching the true public dialogue now necessary in seeking consensus. We are inhibited by a pair of devastating dogmatisms. On the one side, the dogma sits astride a mushroom-shaped cloud; threats of its horror warn that these times do not permit anyone to dedicate his life, only to preserve it. On the other side, the dogma cries treason and iniquity to those who, fearful for their own and humanity's extinction, extend that fear into every other person, and declare that all considerations beyond self-preservation must be abandoned.

To obtain a rational dialogue, dogmas must be set aside. We must discuss, not accuse. The man who differs from us is not the enemy, not on either side. The enemy is the mindless hysteria which prevents reasonable discussion, for never in history has the need for reason and the need for rational decision been so evident. If we, like the peoples of many other nations, arrive at the conclusion that mere biological life outweighs completely the condition of life, then we must act on the basis of just and carefully evaluated consensus, for we will have to pay for that decision with the conditions of all our lives, and our children's lives. If, on the other hand, we arrive at the conclusion that life is worth only its condition, then that determination still must be based on consensus, for we will have to pay for it by risking life itself—as men have paid throughout history, in all their conflicts. Today no kingly or solitary decision can substitute for the consensus; it is not paid or dedicated soldiers who alone will fight and risk in the great decision that will determine the fate of every one of us. Nor can we hedge our bet by hoping that such a consensus would create so much strength of purpose that the conflict symbolized by the mushroom cloud could be avoided. No realism worthy of dedication can be founded on the gambler's easy notion that the hand may never be called. It may be called; it may not be called; but in either case one must face facts accurately and carefully.

Above all, a true dialogue must not become stultified with definitions of any action as "unthinkable."* In rational decision, all existent factors must be "thinkable." To say that new weapons systems make war "unthinkable" is as irrational as saying that new political systems make surrender "unthinkable." Every alternative must be thinkable, and thought about. Otherwise there will be no dialogue, there will be no consensus, and man's fate, whichever way it goes, must risk disaster, for it will be guided by unreason.

The dialogue only begins with the question of survival and values beyond survival. As soon as it exceeds the limits of our era's problem, it must enter into a discussion of values themselves. Neither side must silence the discussion with assumptions. From conditions of life the dialogue must move to conditions of societies, demanding that we know the principals in the conflict which make imperative the deep choices of today. One side must discuss why value choices are meaningless compared to mass survival. The other must explain what values are, and what considerations make them worth dying to preserve or living to fulfill.

Then comes that part of the dialogue that must set

---

*In this context one may applaud the title of a new book by the distinguished physicist and defense analyst, Herman Kahn, *Thinking About the Unthinkable*, Horizon, 1962.

forth details of how these units of discussion mesh, how they may or may not move toward or away from the dreaded conflict. Here, the dialogue must be called upon to discuss, not dogmatize, the patterns in which societies act and interact according to the age-old interplays of power. Without either fear or fanaticism, the dialogue must find out whether new weapons really have created a new behavior, or whether they have merely magnified and intensified old reflexes.

So far the dialogue has been infrequent and usually irrational. Wars that "nobody can win" are freely discussed, but the kinds of wars that *can* be won are often rejected from polite conversation. International power is viewed as proper subject for debate in a world forum, but national power is viewed as improper for discussion even in the nation possessing it. International power is debated in terms of policing and pacifying the world; national power is not discussed in the same way, even though it simultaneously has to be admitted that two nations alone possess the decisive power to create global war or effect global peace. In a rational dialogue, however, we can and must discuss all these things. There is nothing that can be swept under the carpet simply because it is unattractive. The only things that were ever successfully swept under history's carpet were the fragments of those societies which, instead of facing responsibilities or thinking problems through, reacted by closing their minds.

If we cannot discuss, openly and without censure the alternatives of life and death, of war and peace, of power and weakness, of survival, surrenders, and victories—if we must continue to live in a house divided—then the Twentieth century will mark more than our own natural or unnatural deaths. It will mark also our failure to have given that inevitable death a nobility of purpose or even a decent memory of the life that preceded it.

2

BEYOND FREEDOM

IT WILL BE ONLY AFTER we have answered the questions posed by the dialogue that we can form a logical strategy to deal with the perils we face. For strategy must be geared to objectives. Objectives arise from priorities, and priorities from values. The values emerge from an attitude on life itself. Aristotle, one of the earliest as well as one of the greatest practitioners of the dialogue, was as preoccupied by the question of life and its condition as we are today. More than two thousand years ago, he arrived at an answer that centuries have not wearied nor historical crises weakened. Life without a measure of quality, Aristotle said, was worthless.

Towering over the city where Aristotle reasoned, is the temple-topped hill of the Acropolis, symbol of the Hellenic search for form and beauty, the meaning of life. Towering over the cities where the dialogue is being spoken at present, in our own time's search for life's measure of quality, many see a mushroom cloud. It is the contention of one side in today's dialogue that the conditions discerned by Aristotle no longer apply. Those conditions were based upon the willingness of the citizens of Athens to die, if need be, in order that the future freedom of life and mind in Athens might endure. Now, it is said, the central issue is no longer your, or my, or any individual's willingness to sacrifice life to assure the future of those who would survive; for the bomb, we are told, means that no one would survive—not you, not I, not humanity itself. It is said the conflict we face with such dread today would mark not the end of some things to preserve others, but the end of all things. Even values, it is said, die with the people who held them, and those who would take us to the brink of war, take us actually to Armageddon. It is claimed that the antagonists in our modern conflict, are not the Communist Empire and Western civilization, but humanity and nuclear destruction, and that those who fight Communism fight the wrong war against the wrong enemy, for the only real war is humanity against the bomb.

Has Aristotle's sense, then, in our era been made nonsense? Does the bomb now mean that life, even without a measure of quality, is worthwhile so long as it at least inhales and exhales—never mind the poison of the air, the horror of the time? Is the crisis in the heart of the bomb or in the heart of man? These are the supreme questions. Regardless of nation, geographical location, or political party, thoughtful men and women everywhere must face them.

In visits to over fifty college and university campuses during the last two years, I found that many students were tackling these problems. But unfortunately, few scholars today are so addressing themselves, except those scholars who have already decided that the heart of the bomb, not the heart of man, is the problem. Reason is shattered by emotional fission, as soon as nuclear fission is discussed. Impulse, not study, marks the dialogue of the scholars, with few exceptions. But it may be significant that in Munich today, a man whom I have never met and of whom few Americans have even heard, Dr. Eric Voegelin, an exile from Hitler's Germany who taught at Louisiana State and other American universities, has now returned to his homeland and is in the process of publishing a monumental work called *Order and History,* three volumes of which have already appeared. When completed, I believe, it will constitute a pioneer contribution to the dialogue that must develop if humanity is to reason again—an incisive, perceptive examination of history, a basis for viewing the crisis of our time with the perspective our emotions often cause us to reject.

Voegelin sees man's history as a winding path through order and disorder. I believe Voegelin would view atomic war as merely the ultimate—so far—example of disorder. Even so, atomic war is not a novel disorder. For example, in the religious wars of Europe, one-third of its population died. Virtually all the people of the city of Magdeburg, for instance—estimated as some forty thousand—were eliminated in just one of that era's many mass exterminations. There was, in short, a Hiroshima centuries ago, and its devastation was not nuclear nor impelled by materialist ideologies. It was the destruction of Christian fighting Christian—with pikes, swords, and crude muskets. Today's disorder, as Voegelin's study indicates, is not the responsibility of the bomb. It is a disorder of man's spiritual climate and his passions, a disorder that would be familiar to humanity in any age.

Communism has advanced through this disorder, not —as is so often contended—by the strength of its ideas, but by force. Eastern Europe was communized by bayonets; China fell to the coercion of an armed minority; neither event was brought about by the free choice of a majority burning with belief in a new doctrine. It was the disorder surrounding the Second World War that opened the gates to the Communist masters, not the touted key of Communist ideology. It was the disorder of successive revolutions and dictatorships that led to the arrival of the Communist dictatorship which turned Cuba into the garrison state it is today.

The bomb is but a shadowy specter over such events. It has not forced or fed them, but rather has generated fears which have paralyzed many persons who could otherwise have taken preventive action. If we, not just the West, but any and all men interested in the survival of freedom, are to construct a strategy, we must, like Voegelin, study the history of order and disorder. Through such study we may reach conclusions regarding those things worth dying for, living for, and fighting for. The questions asked so far in regard to value have been shallow—for instance, whether greater production of motor cars, or greater public works, or an expanding economy, are of a significance worth dying for in order to protect the nation that has them. When we do get to a basic question, such as freedom, we often find it asked in confusing terms. To some, freedom becomes a negative, the state-idolizing "freedoms from"— freedom from hunger, freedom from fear, and the rest. To others, it becomes the anarchical, positive freedom of limitless choice, regardless of impact on neighbors or community. The first of these answers does not relate to freedom at all, but to paternalistic tyranny; the other is not freedom, but license. The distinguished writer and editor, Max Ways, former chief of the *Time-Life* London bureau, in his brilliant book *Beyond Survival,* aptly termed this type of "freedom from" a "vagabond who hits the road not because he chooses where he is going but because he wants to get out of where he is."* Until very recently, it was the character of the American proposition to steer steadfastly between extremes. When the nation rejected the secure, paternalistic "freedom from" pattern of life it enjoyed as a dependency of the British Crown, it did not revolt into the limitless choice of license. It painfully debated and reasoned its way through the brief historical chaos that marked the period of the Articles of Confederation, until it reached commitment to a constitution of balanced powers and the "right" (but never the guarantee) to the pursuit of happiness. The only guarantee made by the constitutional proposition was that there would be equal treatment before the law, and that individual energy and conscience could be the measure of a man's fulfillment. It was specifically not the tenor of the American proposition to support every other revolution. The American revolution was revolution *for,* revolution characterized by its goals: freedom and equality before the law. Other revolutions, which sought only change and promised only tyranny or anarchy or some other failure of national responsibility, were totally alien to its thinking. There was nothing in the American proposition to prepare anyone for today's most frustrating expression of disorder—a neutralism that demands to be left alone to produce its own chaotic revolutions with no regard for

---

*I recently had the opportunity of visiting with Mr. Ways. In our conversation he reaffirmed his deep concern with the distorted manner in which many of us view freedom. He continued to deplore the misplaced emphasis on "freedom from reality" that is becoming more and more the mark of our times.

responsibilities, either individual or national. This neutralism is not, as it pretends, a rejection of the struggle between major powers; it is a total rejection of responsibility—which is to be borne, meanwhile, by the rest of us.

All men should have freedom, the new catch phrases chant. Some interpret these, as did a recent United Nations resolution, to mean that all colonial territories should immediately be relieved of foreign authority. In fact this resolution stated unequivocally that "inadequacy of political, economic, social or educational preparedness should never serve as a pretext for delaying independence."*

It is a superstition of our time that out of the masses, no matter how disorganized and illiterate they may be, will automatically emerge the civilized state. From this superstition has come, for example, the agony of the Congo. What genuine freedom have the Congolese people, dying by thousands in tribal warfare, coerced by new leaders who have no respect, and indeed no understanding of the concept of freedom which only set them free to prey on the weak? From a similar misapplication of "freedom" in Germany, Hitler emerged. And aided by the same principle of self-determination without self restraint, Hitler was able to demand the Sudetenland in the march of the catastrophic series of events which eventually led to the Second World War.

The American proposition did not sanction this "freedom" for war and chaos, but for the order we call liberty, for the order of individual fulfillment, for the order and responsibility of free institutions, for the order and responsibility of man's eternal pursuit of happiness.

---

*See *United Nations Review,* 1960, p. 49.

Liberty does not, as a rule, emerge from the chaos of revolution; this fact has been proved in all ages. The revolution of France in 1789 brought Napoleon; the revolution of Russia in 1917 brought Lenin, Stalin, and Khrushchev; the revolution of Cuba in 1959 brought Communist dictatorship. Nevertheless, the revolutionary chaos that is often supported today—particularly in a UN dominated by new, unstable nations, often manipulated by Communist countries which violate every precept of the UN charter—this chaos is excused as being in this century what the American Revolution was in its time!

No more tragic misreading of history is imaginable. It is a vicious lie, a "doublespeak" of the type that throughout our era has been a specialty of totalitarians. The pretended similarity does not exist; and in the great dialogue with which we seek the measure that will make modern life worth living, or risking, it is vitally important to understand this: America in 1776 was not at all the same as Asia or Africa in 1962.

Beginning with the Magna Carta, the English Constitution was centuries in the making; wise centuries, responsible centuries, self-controlled centuries—not impatient, unschooled, untried, unbridled, days of violence and nights of terror. Those centuries of representative tradition were already the heritage of the colonists when they settled this land. The Virginia Charter of 1606, for example, provided that the colonists should "have and enjoy all Liberties, Franchises, and Immunities" as though they were abiding in England. The issue was not raised that since they occupied different territories, they should also occupy a separate social order. Because of the distance from the mother country, however, there was added a new responsibility of local government which was easily fulfilled by men who had lived their lives previously in the responsibilities of citizenship.

After the French and Indian Wars, however, the British Crown, then under the dominance at home of the centralizing mercantile philosophy aiming at increasing government control and regulation of all citizens, began to undermine the rights which the colonists had previously held as British subjects. The issue then, and later when the muskets began to blaze, was over the rights of citizenship, of liberty in order. What was sought was not the right to chaos or to license, but to liberty according to concepts that had been developing among free men for centuries. The First and Second Continental Congresses were not assembled to promote revolution, but to end the encroachments upon colonial liberties and to maintain the rights of ordinary citizenship. It took fourteen months for the Second Continental Congress, even after the colonies were aflame with fighting, to decide that severance of ties with the mother country would be needed—*to restore right order,* not to topple it.

More than worlds and years separate that soberly considered, slowly evolved historical decision from the street-prowling incendiary demonstrations of the Twentieth century's so-called "revolutions of rising expectations," (and the clandestine Communist prompting that so often and so easily has conspired to manipulate them). The cry in Ghana was for freedom, but the freedom gained was used to impose a tryranny that ended freedom. The cry in the Congo was for independence, but the independence was used to release tribal hatreds between the warring overlords of terrified and confused peoples. The cry in Cuba was to end corruption and exploitation, but it signalled only the beginning of organized terror, socially ordered starvation, and a hysterical garrison state whose guns were immediately pointed toward every other nation in this hemisphere.

In the American Revolution there was a basis for action as different as decency is from depravity. First, it was a revolution of men committed not to their personal passions or to half-understood abstractions, but to order, to belief in a God beyond history and above government, to pragmatic respect for governments long established, and to the belief that such government should not be changed for light reasons. The independence movement of the Thirteen States came only after long and patient suffering, and it came only when it was ascertained that the King intended to establish a tyranny. It was not a movement impelled by mere covetousness of land or riches; it was not powered by a people ignorant of the world and of history, but by men long cultured and educated in the responsibilities of liberty. And in their resolve they appealed to a whole system of established ethics, to Him they called upon as Supreme Judge of the world. They pledged not only their physical lives and their material fortunes, but also their honor, a concept fully recognized and held sacred. These values, these commitments beyond the physical or merely material, did not rise among positivistic men who thought truth was relative, but among men who believed in self-evident and eternal verities. Honor was a measure more important than mere survival. How they lived was more important than whether they lived.

They had been unwilling to destroy the order under which they had lived. Thus when the pinnacle of that order, the Crown itself, had destroyed the very principles that gave that order validity, they undertook a revolution to preserve the liberty already known and understood—not to shatter order and substitute disorder. There was, in the concept of the American Revolution, only one place for a freedom *from* anything—freedom from power wielded without restraint. The remainder of the concept was concerned with freedoms *to:* to enjoy rights of privacy, to pursue one's own ends, and to maintain the related responsibilities and privileges of free men under a free government. There was no concept of freedom from poverty, for instance, but there was a strong concept of the freedom to prosper by and according to one's own lights and energy. In the present chaotic revolutions of so-called rising expectations, however, the freedoms *from* are too often little more than freedoms from reality, from the harsh and sometimes hard responsibilities of life, from responsibility for individual fulfillment. Substituted for the idea of responsibility is the idea of group fulfillment and state security. Government direction takes the place of individual direction, "planning" is praised instead of purpose, coercion replaces conscience.

In another of his works, *The New Science of Politics*, Eric Voegelin, the historian whose contribution was mentioned earlier as important in initiating the new dialogue of values, warns of the nation which elevates its politics, its government programs, to a rank that in another day would be reserved to God, and which uses the pretence of group salvation as a means of escaping individual responsibility. Christ said, render unto Caesar things which are Caesar's and unto God things that are God's. There was no inherent inner conflict for the early Christians living under the temporal authority of Caesar, and simultaneously under the divine compulsion of their God. The conflict came externally and then passed within, when the empire began its attempts to deify Caesar, to clothe a man with the mantle of God. Today governments in every quarter of the globe are more and more claiming the prescience and power of gods on earth and inevitably stress of every description is arising from the anomaly.

All men of course crave security, and often they tend to deify the sources of security. In more primitive cultures this could mean the deification of great leaders, or the land's fertility, or sun, or the sea. To modern man it too often means deification of the state. For today's superstition is that the state can offer security, whether through the autocratic impositions of a Caesar Augustus, or an Adolph Hitler, or a party elite.

The Socialist system, for instance, claims to supply security to every man according to his needs, taking in return only what his abilities make it possible for him to perform—the famous formula maintained most notably by Karl Marx. But to assure this security, the state must own every major means to the creation of wealth; and wealth is the tool of society's advance. And, of course, the state must possess the power to frame policy, that makes it possible to preserve this ownership and order its use. This ownership, the argument goes, is ownership by all the people, although—only for pure efficiency's sake of course—a *few* of the people have to do the actual managing and be, in effect, the active owners. To achieve efficiency, these managers must have the absolute and unending power to enforce their will. Thus they become in fact the god-masters of the state and of the people. No matter how noble their purposes, their system rests upon the one condition that liberty always has most abhorred—the absolute concentration of power, unbalanced, unappealable power.

Some measure of security such a system may possibly guarantee. But never liberty, and never even security beyond the purely physical measures of distributing calories and housing. It cannot provide the interior security that strengthened Ghandi, fasting in the prisons of India, risking his life and utilizing a moral imperative in the attempt to bring others to an understanding of principles before taking peaceful action to secure them. It cannot provide the security of Polycarp, Bishop of Smyrna, as he stood ready to die at the hands of Rome's executioners, rather than deny Christ and swear allegiance to the cult of the Roman State. These men fought for an inner integrity that no social security or medical care program ever could provide, a housing loan enshrine, or a corporate vice-presidency afford. This is not to make the absurd claim that material needs can be ignored; Ghandi wanted a higher standard of living for India's people. The bearing of the proposition is far deeper—that material security or material benefit can be deified only at the risk of losing the values that make life meaningful.

We have infinitely compounded the anxieties of modern man by the myth of a materialistic utopia. Without the consistency of right and just action, which can be provided only by strength of spirit, even the utopia of materialism vanishes as the newly deified masters seize more and more privilege for themselves. Deadened is the role of personal charity and responsibility. In our own American version of the materialist utopia, we have distorted the role of government and of citizens in helping people to help themselves, but, more important, we have given a false response in the great dialogue of our age. Security of soul comes from the freedom to search for and find meaning in reality, to build meaning into a political order which can preserve over the years values more important than the merely physical. It is the security which comes out of order in the soul, order reflecting meaning beyond life, that alone can create order in any sphere of life, including the material. The American Revolution was founded in this search for meaning, based on eternal, self-evident truths upon which men were willing to stake their sacred honor, regretting that they had but one life to give. The Constitution was a reflection of certain divine truths—that God created man in his own image, that man is not divine, nor is he to play God—hence he must have in his political order a strong system of checks and balances.

The impact of the Declaration of Independence and the Constitution resulted not solely from the abstract imaginings of Washington, Jefferson, Hamilton, Madison, and Franklin, but from their ability to capture real truths; that is, to comprehend and cope with reality. There were grave problems for the strong leadership of those days—inexperienced generals made mistakes, our Continental Congress fumbled, hundreds of knaves dodged military service, cheats got rich from war, one-third of the colonists did not even support the Revolution, and another third were Tories. Our present leadership and especially our present Congressional participation has also been of superior quality. Why then our brilliant success in the earlier era contrasted to our recent tragic failures?

The answer is—as the Founding Fathers would say—self-evident. We have not grasped real truth in our time; we have not developed a meaningful dialogue to fit our problem; and our policies, lacking in grasp of the true realities, have therefore also lacked direction and consistency. The political order of our nation has been allowed to crumble until we react and think in the hysteria of a supposedly abnormal and perpetual emergency, while the truth is that humanity and nations have always faced emergency. National policy often has become geared only to the animal response of mere survival, not to the truths beyond nature, which alone make survival both possible and meaningful. For years, colonial leaders such as George Washington debated whether to break off from the Crown, but with the Declaration of Independence behind him, Washington did not hesitate in his strike against the Hessians at Trenton. We, however, were notably without such guiding purpose in the early morning hours of April 17, 1961 when, having committed ourselves to a line of action in Cuba, we suddenly faltered, betrayed our allies, withdrew air support, and produced a failure which shook American prestige throughout the world.

It was not that we had no precedent, or principle for action in such a case. The Monroe Doctrine was a well accepted principle for decades, one which offered historical and legal authority even for direct and unilateral intervention. The noted diplomatic historian, Professor Samuel Flagg Bemis, as early as December 1959, had set forth the way for quick United States action against the invasion of International Communism in countries such as Cuba. He rested his case on a series of historical precedents—the Monroe Doctrine of 1823; the Gettysburg Address; the 1940 Act of Havana; the Inter-American Treaty of Reciprocal Assistance, 1947; the Declaration of Washington, 1951; the Declaration of Caracas, 1954. And yet on that April day when we faced the Cuban crisis, we did not feel we had the moral strength to use power for the security of the Americas; we did not feel that the fate of the Cuban people under Communism was anyone's concern but their own; and so we submerged both our own national security and the decency of our internal moral order in the morass of guilt complexes, which led to the basing of minimum strategic requirements upon a hazy concept of world popularity—instead of on truth, principle and established order which alone wins either respect or popularity.

There will be critics who will answer that this analysis looks too deep, that the sole explanation was a new, inexperienced president plagued by even more inexperienced advisors. But the colonists, too, were inexperienced. The difference was that they had an outlook based upon real, everlasting truth which gave them purpose and conviction despite flagrant tactical blunders —such as the Battle of Long Island, to cite only one. Nor did this type of breakdown in order come with this Administration.

While the previous Administration in actual operation never permitted a disaster comparable to Cuba, nevertheless it allowed itself to be circumscribed by limitations imposed by a wrong view of the modern problem. For example, John Foster Dulles, certainly not inexperienced, had a grasp of truth, and the strength of his moral convictions irked many Americans, especially those who believed everything was relative. Anyone who hopes for the unflinching practice of moral criteria must admire Dulles' sincerity. His conviction, firmness and moral strength were time and again demonstrated in the firm stands and the willingness to meet force with force that both he and President Eisenhower displayed in Lebanon, Quemoy-Matsu, Vietnam, Korea and Guatemala. Yet, in June of 1953, even John Foster Dulles faltered at the time of the East German uprisings, when he rejected—on moral as well as practical grounds—the use of our overwhelming power to help a struggling, agonized people set themselves free. The supposed morality was that we had no right to intervene—and, beyond that, no right to risk World War III, although now it appears highly doubtful that such risk existed.

In 1953 and again in Hungary in 1956, it was a moral inhibition that prescribed our lack of action. What we in fact were showing in all these cases was not moral order at all, but our immoral and suicidal willingness to act as if there were Communist legitimacy no matter how baseless. What our inaction proclaimed to the world was that we do not see that the Communist way is an affront to man's nature and to God, nor that it is moral to use power against it. In these and many other cases—in Korea, Suez, Asia, and Africa—we are ceaselessly trapped in our reactive, fragmented foreign policy, in which our power is not used meaningfully, in which our people find no compelling motivation—only animal existence, glorified materialism, growthmanship, and devitalizing bureaucracy.

The crisis is deep and dangerous. Walter Lippmann once spoke of the need for a public philosophy, but he and most of those like him seem themselves to have succumbed to the despair of the times and lost their vitality.

Such ideas are now seldom propounded. Yet our crisis can be solved only by a public strategy,* a reconstruction out of the broken pieces of failure, a positive policy for which men will both die and live, ultimate values which make sense from nonsense.

The foundation of this public strategy must go back to the very roots of the philosophy of the West, to Aristotle's concept that we seek a life to be lived under certain conditions, that these conditions spring from the truths such as those that our Founding Fathers found self-evident. The most self-evident truth of all is that man must have freedom to find and choose his God, and under God fulfill his destiny through developing God's gifts. No man under God can think of himself alone. In freedom for personal creativity man must allow for his fellow man and for his community. One man's liberty must not destroy another man's freedom. Government must be limited—strong government, but also strongly limited. For the sake of justice, constitutions are written for the naive as well as for the wise. Ideally we want for all countries constitutional government, but the ideal may in some cases be impossible, or capable only of gradual evolution. But our measure of all governments should be, meanwhile, the degree of freedom they offer the individual. Franco's Spain may offer more freedom to the individual, for example, than some governments operating under the guise of democracy, but actually performing as a tyranny. Ghana is one such example.

Our nation must recall the essential element of for-

---

*The concept of a public strategy is taken from "Fundamentals of a National Strategy," by Dr. David M. Abshire, reprinted in the remarks of Rep. Gerald R. Ford (R-Mich.), *Congressional Record*, June 20, 1960.

eign policy which our forefathers understood. If governments derive their just powers from the consent of the governed, then the obligation of the government is first and foremost to the governed. Here justice and national interest coincide, and here is the source of the confusion in our current foreign policy. Much of our foreign policy today does not serve our interest or the world's interest, but subordinates itself to something called "world opinion", or to any majority position of the United Nations, often hindering our national rights and the human rights of the majority of the world's populations. For the real interest of the United States today coincides with the real interests of humanity— peace functioning under justice and order, where all men can freely seek their personal destinies, and can pursue their own happiness. This creative but orderly evolution must be the ultimate aim of public strategy; for diametrically opposed to it stands the Communist goal of keeping society chained, cowering, closed in tyranny; and, in direct contravention to Communism's professed ideology, crush the many who are ruled, to benefit the few who rule—a system of exploitation whose equal in ruthlessness the world has never seen.

3

THE COMMUNISTS AND WAR*

FOR AN EFFECTIVE and meaningful dialogue more is
needed than a discussion of our own values. Communist
values, Communist theory, and Communist attitudes
must also enter the dialogue, be discussed, and become
part and parcel of the factors that precede consensus on
policy and strategy.

Dr. Robert Strausz-Hupé, the director of the Foreign
Policy Research Institute at the University of Pennsylvania, has said that the Communists "are armed" with
the "Marxist-Leninist theory of revolution (and that)
this theory is in many ways obsolete (and) many of its
conclusions are wrong."† "Yet," he said, "it is a coherent
theory of historical process—and it does give insight,
limited and dogmatic though it may be—into the nature

---

*Gerhart Niemeyer, Professor of Political Science at the University
of Notre Dame, lecturer at the National War College, and author of
many articles and books on Communism, has undertaken a study of
Communist philosophy and teachings that seeks to go back before Marx
and Engels to the personalities and ideas that gave rise to the Communist ideology. I am deeply indebted to Dr. Niemeyer for the many
hours he has spent discussing with me the Communists and their attitude towards war.

†From a recent speech. In a discussion I had later with Dr. Strausz-
Hupé, he confirmed the view.

of the world struggle and the problem before mankind."

To peoples of the Western world war always has been a simply defined condition. If nations were shooting at, or marching against one another, that was called war. If they were not, that was peace, no matter how uneasy.

The Communist empire, however, has developed an entirely new lexicon. War is not the absence of peace. Peace, in fact, may be one of war's conditions. War, in the Communist lexicon, is the entire span of time and range of tactics involved in reducing the non-Soviet world to helplessness and, finally, to subjugation. To the Communist, this state of affairs is praiseworthy and desirable. The Communist says that the "true" social order cannot be realized throughout the globe until the entire process of material production and consumption has been collectivized. According to Marxist doctrine, man's nature results from his relation to the products of his labor, and man cannot be his "true" or collective self if his labor contributes to anyone's private property, even his own. Hence the Communist is in fierce and self-righteous rebellion against what he regards as the present false, hypocritical political order which is keeping man from realizing his true self. The only social force capable of destroying this false order and redeeming mankind is said to be the Communist Party, the vanguard of the proletariat, which must war against the present order until it is destroyed and replaced by a social system that will not—as this one avowedly does— set up a special interest over the whole society. Human life then for the first time will be lived in the unity and harmony of the world-wide collective. Until this is achieved, the Communist must engage in struggle, a war on all levels.

There are, of course, many ways of regarding this struggle which are more pleasing to the West. Most pleasant is the notion that this isn't a conflict situation at all—it is a competition. In this view, the Communist base, the Soviet Union, is regarded merely as the nation which threw off Czarist tyranny and emerged from an agricultural social structure to become an industrial, if state controlled, nation. Despite occasional regrettable harshness—no greater, really, these sympathizers claim, than the harshness of America's own early days of development and exploitation—the Russian nation's experiment in socialism is working miraculously well, and now challenges the United States to prove that it has anything better to offer the world, which by choosing sides will decide the outcome of the competition. This version of the situation in the West is notably welcomed by Mr. Khrushchev, who frequently refers to it.

In this description it is said that the Soviet Union's open belligerence—for example, its hold by force on the nations along its European border—is justified by natural and simple fears of aggression against Russia by the Germans, or by war-mongers in America and in other nations panicked by the successful growth of the peaceful Communist peoples as they pursue their great experiment. Virtually all evaluations of the Soviet situation, with the exception of those which arrive at a view of the Soviet Union as a purposeful, persistent aggressor, waging a real war in new ways, are merely extensions of one or more aspects of the concept just described.

On the other side are those who hold that the situation between ourselves and the Soviet Union is actual war, not competition or even uneasy peace; that it is the onslaught of a will to dominance, not the harmonious advance of a great idea. That it is a crisis in the history of civilizations; not merely a clash of social and economic theories. Those who hold to this belief are at every step opposed to the thinking of those who regard Communism simply as the great competition. In the words of Charles Malik, the philosopher-statesman from Lebanon, former President of the UN General Assembly, "what is at stake in this war is the traditional view of man, society, history, truth and God which the Mediterranean-European-Western world has painstakingly developed over four thousand years of history."*

Those who agree with Mr. Malik and see the Soviet Union as an aggressive, warlike force bent upon dominating all tradition and every society, point out that in actual fact the Soviet leadership did not even overthrow Czarist tyranny. On the contrary, what the Communist leadership actually overthrew was the constitutional and genuinely democratic government of Alexander Kerensky, who represented the popular forces which toppled the Czar. Since then Communism has never once received any free majority mandate that could be cited to show that it has the consent of the persons it controls. As a Socialist state it is patterned after the state-power complexes of Fascist (Socialist) Italy and Nazi (Socialist) Germany, not after the mixed-socialist, private-enterprise forms of Great Britain, New Zealand, or Sweden, to which proponents of the great competition

---

*From a recent speech by Mr. Malik. The view has been confirmed at other times in private discussion, as has my personal respect for Mr. Malik's keen and scrupulous intellect.

view prefer to compare it. Secondly, the Soviet Union's exploitation of its people bears no resemblance to the economic imbalances that marked the American emergence from an agricultural to an industrial society. No rational comparison is possible, for instance, between the ante-bellum plantation system and the collectivized Ukrainian farms. In the Ukraine Nikita Khrushchev directed the mass extermination by execution and planned starvation of a population which the most modest estimates place at ten million persons. Furthermore, the notion that the Soviet Union is counting on peaceful "conversion" of the world to Communism—a necessary corollary if the peaceful competition view is to be accepted—must smash against the harsh fact that not a single nation, not even the Russian Socialist base itself, has ever been freely "converted" to Communist domination. The entire alphabet of Soviet conquest—Albania, Bulgaria, Czechoslovakia, and the rest—has been written by bayonets, not even once by free ballots.

In addition, those who contend that fear of aggression by West Germany makes excusable the Soviet enslavement of the nations around its borders must take into consideration the following hard fact: the organization of West Germany's armed force, by design, is such that it is incapable of taking aggressive action without the support of the United States. Thus, in order to accept the theory that the Russians are afraid of the German remnant, one must also think the Russians believe that this country is eager for aggression and for World War III and will commit itself to support of a nation whose weakness it has deliberately ensured. People who can regard that as reasonable are beyond the point of being able to engage in rational dialogue.

In point of fact, nearly all the further contentions of the peaceful competition view lack rationality. It is said that the Soviet Union offers underdeveloped nations a new way to industrialize, one which must terrify us—weary and declining industrialists that we are. In actuality, however, the Soviet Union is not yet itself a consistently industrialized nation, even after two generations of forced labor. To feed the Russian people, half the Soviet population must still remain bound to the soil on the collective farms. Even so, one-third of the vaunted industrial production of the Soviet empire does not even come from the industry of Russia, but must be forcibly imported from the captive nations.

Thus, can it be *what* the Soviet has to offer that is the key to conflict? Or is it *how* they are offering it? The "how" is the real issue behind all the polite debating at conference tables and cocktail parties.

The Soviet "how" is represented by such means as political assassination, subversion, covert warfare, blackmail, guerilla forays, armed suppression of subject peoples, and the international structure of the fifth column. It is these *means,* not the theoretical *ends* of Communism that keep the world in its present state of tension. The one theoretical concept, essential to the motive power of the Soviet-based conflict is that of "historical inevitability." This is the concept which places the Soviet leaders and their adherents beyond reach of reason. They believe with irrational, fanatical zeal that the Communist Party, wherever in the world it exists, is the legitimate and inevitable representative of the mass of the people and that, no matter what the means necessary, it must in the end become the sole political organization on earth. All parties opposed to the Com-

munist Party are history's enemy. History will sweep
them away. Any help given to history, therefore, is
proper and right. It is impossible to imagine a vision
more opposite to the traditional Western view of war as
a clash between two or more nations whose specific
interests are involved—such interests as boundaries or
the status of the ruling group in one or the other of the
nations, or overseas possessions, domination of trade
routes, ports, and the rest. And certainly the notion of
peaceful competition becomes absurd.

Today our traditional view is split. On the one hand,
it seems to be concerned with the problem of preventing
further Soviet incursions into the free world's territory,
and the intent to remain militarily strong is based upon
this goal. At the same time, however, our strength is
dedicated to preventing a war; a war which, it is in-
cessantly claimed, "could literally mean the end of
civilization," and, therefore, even while we arm we
must speak of disarmament, look ahead to it, dream of
it, and indulge in wishful thinking which completely
ignores facts. We have, as Admiral Arleigh Burke has
ironically pointed out, balanced our Department of Defense by creating a separate Disarmament Agency. Certainly we have a disarmament frame of mind.

The two preoccupations are of course incompatible.
On one hand, the United States issues statements about
not yielding more territory to Communism, proclaiming
our intent of "containing" it within the vast empire it
already has carved. On the other hand, we seek to prevent the use of force anywhere in the world—even by
ourselves. The first of those preoccupations involves the
traditional power concepts, traditional protections of
boundaries which cannot always, or even often be

protected without resorting to force. But our dedication to the United Nations—a far different sort of dedication than that of the Soviet Union to this same organization —precludes the use of force. The result, as could be anticipated, is Western immobility and indecision, and the fatal duality whose growing articulation, even by policy makers, is that war, not the Soviet Union, is the enemy. As a majority articulation of public opinion in the Free World, this would inevitably mean "peace at any price."

Communists, on the other hand, have a far more effective approach to the conflict. Their dogma commits them to an approach which recognizes the self-evident truth of warfare—the ruthlessly realistic understanding that one side will win, the other lose. Nevertheless, from any salutary *fear* that they may lose, the Communists are insulated by an irrational conviction that history is on their side and opposing political institutions are doomed. One cannot "peacefully compete" with such people. One cannot even argue with them. What one must do, however, is make sure that their irrationality does not destroy our own power to think.

We must freely face facts as they exist. For example, the forward flow of Communism is not limited by geography, although the Soviet Communist Party is the home party and the Soviet Union is the homeland. But Communism itself ranges without regard to borders. In Communist strategic formulations, it is possible to conclude that, given sufficient incentive, Communists would be willing to sacrifice even the homeland, if, in return, they could be sure of emerging with a world situation which would allow their movement to proceed more effectively to gobble up opposing political units. In a conventional war, for instance, it might be quite feasible from the point of view of dedicated Communists, to permit the Soviet Union to sustain crushing blows from the Free World if, at the same time, external Communist Parties could be assured that, in the wake of the struggle, they could take over the majority of the non-Soviet nations. The physical destruction of the Soviet Union would leave as heirs the Red Chinese and the entrenched machines of the captive nations, and the poised and organized Communist Parties in every nation beyond the Iron Curtain. Communism, although Soviet based, is thus a total political reality, worldwide, and with the ultimate goal of destruction of all competing structures—destruction to be achieved by any means and at any time, under the ringing historical justification of the "inevitable triumph of history." In spite of their occasional differences, these people have the essential unity of all irrational believers who act.

For believers, what is the function of war? Communist doctrine leaves no doubt. War is merely one more justifiable means of hastening the end of the historical process. It is a means to be used, however, only when it cleary risks little if any chance of total Communist defeat. On a limited scale it may perhaps be used when lesser pressures cannot prevent some opposition action that threatens Communism, but the proper situation is one which presents overwhelming odds for victory. Thus the irrational belief of Communism's adherents is combined with the most realistic regard of strategy. It is difficult to find, anywhere in Communist writings on strategy, even a hint that Communism would, in the manner of a completely irrational dictatorship such as Hitler's, launch a Götterdämerung in response to Western action.

With irrational belief in historical inevitability, combined with rational recognition of superior physical force, there is little question that the realistic Communist decision, if confronted by odds against victory, would be to withdraw from the field and plan for future opportunity, rather than risk their own physical extinction. Communists, like some of their friends in the West, prefer not to end up dead. In their materialistic philosophy, death is the end of the line, and all major Communist policy indicates a sincere desire to avoid nuclear war at present. The impulse, however, is not humanitarian as in the West; it is purely realistic. It is understood that, at the present stage of weaponry, they would lose such a war. It is the losing, not the warring, that they consider intolerable. Today's priority is given, therefore, to warfare of the type now waged against us in Viet Nam and Laos, as well as to psychological, political and—where feasible—economic warfare.

In this context it is imperative to recognize the goal of Soviet strategy. This goal is control over situations—not merely over real estate. Soviet writings on strategy show the fear of losing control over situations to be far greater than fear of loss of territory, an attitude the West has completely misunderstood, sacrificing much of its own situational control for momentary advantages which turned out to be purely geographic. The settlement of the war in Korea is an example. The United States and its allies managed to salvage a certain amount of real estate, but by the indecisive truce, even though we held the preponderance of power, we gave situational control into the hands of the Communists. In their goal of securing maximum situational manipulation, the Communists have developed an ideal tool, sublimited warfare, the highly specialized guerilla-type attack now being mounted against us in Asia. Sublimited warfare is an offspring of the post World War II concept of "limited war," in which it was held that troops of the two opposing giant world forces might find themselves in conflict in a limited geographical area, with limited weapons. Sublimited warfare adds the further refinement—extremely convenient to the Soviet Union—that actual Soviet troops need not be called upon at all. Warfare will be waged by propagandizing and terrorizing native populations, by playing upon so-called anti-colonialism, by alliance with local Communist parties, or merely nationalist parties which the Communists will infiltrate. Sublimited warfare is at present a far more effective and safer device from the Soviet point of view than any form of conventional warfare, however limited. Conventional warfare, even in a geographically contained area, could escalate toward actual nuclear war—at this time more devastating for the Soviets than for us. Thus, in terms of realistic Soviet thinking, rather than in the irrational belief in ultimate victory, it would be a major loss of situational control—one not to be risked.

Communist attitudes underlying the Berlin situation are similar, and in the West are similarly misunderstood. The Communists do not envision any settlement of the situation, but want simply to keep control of it—a means to an end. Dr. Stefan T. Possony, co-author of *A Forward Strategy for America,* and presently affiliated with the Hoover Institution on War, Revolution and Peace at Stanford University, has emphasized, on several occasions the Communist stress on *control* of situations. In his analysis of Khrushchev's policy speech of January 6, 1961, for instance, Dr. Possony said: "Khrushchev is not interested in solving the Berlin problem *per se. . . .*

Berlin is an opportunity for offensive Communist action, just as, in 1939, the Polish corridor offered an opportunity for Nazi political action."

The West views the Berlin situation differently—as an end in itself, a sore spot in the world that could be healed, if only the Communists at one time and place would agree to certain rules. That they could easily abandon the rules tomorrow is not considered as important as the idea that they might obey them for a moment or two. Such agreement, it is felt by some Western diplomats, might get the Soviets into a habit of being civilized about such matters. Walt Whitman Rostow, Chairman of the Policy Planning Council in the State Department, displayed this type of optimism on the television program, *Meet the Press,* in May of 1962. In answer to a question about our containment policy, Mr. Rostow replied,

. . . in the long run we are heartened by the trends inside the Communist bloc and the performance of the Communists where they have achieved power. We think the longer-run forces at work in the world are working our way. So that in containing, we are developing positively the whole of the free world, using our influence to do so, and we are looking beyond to work with the forces which may in time emerge within the Communist bloc to make the world a place that more nearly conforms to the criteria that we all signed onto in the U.N. Charter.

Naive thinking of this type has been baseless for two generations. Such optimism about Hitler was abandoned in a matter of months. However, the surface realisms of the Communists have to some observers given an effect of rationality which has made their basic irrationality harder to recognize. Even when faced with demonstrated Communist ruthlessness obviously as insane as Nazi Germany's, many in the West still prefer to look for "signs of change" in Soviet behavior, even though there has been no credible instance demonstrating a basic change of Communist doctrine since its initial assault against freedom when it overthrew the democratic regime of Alexander Kerensky and established the first great base of Communist tyranny. One may even cite, for example, a statement by President Kennedy made in a speech on foreign policy delivered at the University of California on March 23, 1962:

The prospect of a partnership with the Soviet scientists in the exploration of space opens up exciting prospects of collaboration in other areas of learning. And cooperation in the pursuit of knowledge can hopefully lead to cooperation in the pursuit of peace.

The West misunderstands two prime Communist principles. The first is the concept of "Communist fluidity," according to which trained Communists are told now, as from the beginning, that they must be "flexible," that is: feel perfectly free to employ means entirely inconsistent with Communist ends. For example, nationalist movements in Asia must be championed—as a move toward eventual destruction of that same nationalism. Similarly, capitalistic institutions are to be used—to destroy capitalism. The second and related principle is the distinction made by trained Communists between strategy and tactics. Strategy is determined by the over-all direction of attack, the main blow at any particular stage of the world revolution; strategy therefore follows a defined plan. Tactics, on the other hand, are not defined; they adapt themselves to each ebb and flow in the revolutionary tide.

Today Soviet Russia and Red China are locked in debate only over what *tactics* to follow in this stage of world revolution. It is absurd to believe that this dispute indicates any basic cleavage. Disagreements over tactics have pervaded the history of International Communism since its inception, just as they affected—but never destroyed—internal Communism within Russia. As early as the Second Congress of the Comintern, Stalin and R. V. Roy, the Indian delegate, bitterly fought over Stalin's assertion that the proper tactic was to forget temporarily the internal revolution in Asian countries in order to support nationalism in its war against western imperialism. Tactical arguments that have emerged in the past between Soviet and Red Chinese leaders have always been resolved in one way or the other in the pattern of the Marxist dialectic—as soon as one side prevailed, the whole body of International Communism achieved synthesis on a higher level of the strategic end—world domination.

What beclouds reason in the West is the diversity in the means of pursuing the changeless doctrinal goal. Whereas, Hitler always chose the brute routes of force, Communism is as much at home with propagandizing through cultural exchange as it is with midnight murder. Communism can with perfect equanimity proceed from protestations of peace to megaton rattles of anger. Instead of asking, "what do they mean?" the West should ask, "what do they want?" The answer to that reaches the basic issue and never changes—they want the world.

Even as our ally in World War II, Communism merely suspended its openly anti-Western activities in order to help destroy its own rival in totalitarianism. It was not the nature of Hitlerism that repelled Communism, but its power. Had Hitler won, Communism would have been burned out at its then indispensable base in the Soviet Union.

The lesson becomes even clearer when one considers postwar "peaceful coexistence." Many men have reasoned that Khrushchev is different, that he doesn't want war, that he truly believes in "peaceful competition and coexistence." It was at the Twentieth Party Congress in 1956 that he is supposed to have deeply shocked the Communist world by giving renewed hope in some quarters of the free world in the announcement that war was no longer "inevitable," and that the communization of the globe could be accomplished by "peaceful competition." Actually, the meaning of "peaceful competition," the temporary lull needed to make worldwide Communism industrially omnipotent, was clear in the minds of all Communists, while Khruschev created the illusion of sincerity in the naive traditionalists of the West who accepted his words at face value according to their own Western vocabularies. Mr. Khruschev's use of the term "peaceful competition," was merely one more application of Communist fluidity, and beneath the apparently rational surface, the irrational fanaticism advanced. All existing order continues to be bludgeoned by onslaughts of Communism; and so it will be, until from the ultimate complete destruction of order, it is foreseen that world Communism will emerge victorious.

Western misunderstanding of Communist irrationalism—a misunderstanding itself irrational—goes a long way toward explaining the great strides Communism has

made, its long succession of victories over the free world
in the relatively short period of Communist history.
Communism is an irrational force, but the effect it has
on those who observe it without insight is one of purest
realism—and so its inner rationality is assumed. Communism is an atheistic philosophy of world dominance,
with naked privilege for the rulers, outer darkness for
the ruled, but the effect it has on its followers makes it
seem a selfless religion—a religion of materialism and
without God, but one with great appeal.

Khrushchev's goal is to further the cause of Communism in every conceivable way. He believes in its ultimate triumph even though he does not expect to live
to see it. In this respect Communism is indeed a religion,
and the leaders of the movement are quite sincere in its
realistic propagation. Khrushchev believed what he said
when he remarked to the American Senators: "Your
grandchildren will live under Socialism." At the same
time he was quite aware of the strategic value of the
statement as propaganda. On such occasions, the irrational core and the realistic surface meet in their mutual
reinforcement.

The basic philosophy of Communism is adhered to
by all Communists, and all are committed to the same
objective, the ultimate triumph of world Communism.
Here is where they have their most distinct tactical
advantage over the West; they have a purpose and an
ultimate objective which serves as the guiding principle
for all that they do; in short, a public philosophy. Although their tactics change, the doctrine remains constant. Every action is directed toward achievement of
their one goal.

Immediately after the Second World War, the Communists began again in earnest where they had left off a few short years before. In 1946, Stalin made it clear that any cooperation between the Soviet Empire and the "Imperialist Powers" that had come about through wartime expediency and mutual need was ended, and that Communism would again in the name of historical inevitability launch its offensive against all non-Communist nations by whatever means became available. From that day to the present, the Communist Empire has expanded in a more imperialistic fashion than any so-called "imperialist" power in history. The absolutism of its Empire extends from East Germany to Red China and includes as satellites, Albania, Poland, Tibet, Bulgaria, North Korea, North Vietnam, Hungary, Rumania, Yugoslavia, the Baltic States, and Czechoslovakia. Close to fulfillment seems Stalin's prediction that, although encircled by capitalism, the day was not far off when the Soviet Empire would encircle the capitalist nations. As long ago as 1958, Khrushchev remarked in an interview that appeared in the French paper, *Le Figaro*: "I would like to draw your attention to the fact that at present the concept of 'capitalistic encirclement' of our country itself seriously needs a more accurate definition. With the formation of the world system of socialism, the situation in the world has altered radically, and it has not altered, as you know, to the advantage of capitalism. At present it is not known who encircles whom. The Socialist countries cannot be considered as some kind of an island in a rough capitalist sea." Khrushchev's pronouncement marked the prime objective of present-day Soviet policy —the consolidation of the Soviet satellites and the acquisition of such territories as would most readily enable the Communist Empire to surround and ultimately extinguish all non-Communism.

Because the Second World War left Germany and Japan prostrate at the feet of the victorious Allies, and further, because Great Britain, France, and Italy were greatly weakened by the ravages of the conflict, the post-war era found the Soviet Union the strongest nation on the continent and the second strongest in the world. The first step of postwar Soviet strategy was to weld Hungary, Bulgaria, Albania, Czechoslovakia, and Rumania into a solid bloc under complete control of Soviet autocracy. With this accomplished, Communist strategy turned to the Middle East and Southeast Asia, to play on the nationalist tendencies and underdeveloped status of those countries in such a way as to bring them into the Communist orbit.

The United States and the Western powers have not been entirely idle: they moved into Korea and fought a "police action," executed the Berlin airlift, moved naval forces into Lebanon—in short whenever geography appeared threatened by overt acts of aggression, America and the powers of the West moved in to preserve boundaries. In addition, repeated attempts were made to "negotiate" with the Communists and convince them of the West's sincere desire for peace. The unvarying failure of these endeavors is now a matter of historical record.

Does Communism necessarily have to remain true to its core of irrational dogma? Is there really no room for the comforting hope that Khrushchev is a more reasonable man than Stalin or Mao Tse-Tung? The hard fact is that Communism will always remain true to its core because it has no choice. If the basic tenets of Communism were altered or even modified, the whole Communist Empire would collapse. The hard core of Communist doctrine is the foundation of every government, every institution, and every system of rule in the Soviet Empire. Remove any part of this foundation and chaos would result. If the Communists ceased to view the West irrationally, as a war-monger, what justification would the Communist masters have for maintaining their autocratic privileges in their garrison state in Russia? Or in China?

Communism can abandon no part of its basic attitudes. Without the dialectic of historical necessity promising the inevitability of Communist victory, the heart would go out of the overburdened peoples; the thirst for their human rights would become unquenchable. Without the ruthless doctrine of ends and means, the Communist rulers could not pursue the strategy which brings them victories. Without the maintenance of atheism, they could not enforce the sacrifices which maintain their own power in the deified state. Communism cannot change; and to believe in the possibility of change is a madness almost as far from the true ordering of reason as the ideology itself. Communism, while it exists, must remain what it is. It is caught up in the most vicious circle in human history.

4
—

THE UNDERDOG STRATEGY

FROM THE ENORMOUS QUANTITY of secret and unclassified testimony given to my Committee* in Congress, it is unmistakably clear that the United States has a four-to-one superiority over the Soviet Union in nuclear weapons and in the ability to deliver destructive power. It is also clear that the United States has not yet developed a sense of its strength, or of its meaning in terms of international strategy—in terms of keeping the peace in the only way it can now be kept, by reducing to impotence the ability of the Soviet Union aggressively to force its irrational drive to dominance upon the world. That ability, the facts say at every point, is an ability of will, rooted in the superior Russian determination, not in superior technology, society, culture, or weapons.

We, and the West which we lead, have been following a strategy seemingly based upon an attitude of no superiority at all, an attitude even of inferiority. The tragic ineptitude of the defeatist assumption that we are underdogs has led us to take steps that tend to make that supposedly inferior position real. It now seems very probable that our long delay in getting on with the testing of nuclear weapons may have given the Soviet

---

*House Defense Appropriations Subcommittee.

48

Union an unchallenged period of time in which to press ahead with their research and eventually enable them to surpass us, an objective they could have reached in no other way except through our own fearful paralysis of will and suicidal suspension of nerve.

In the strategic equation, time is not on our side, for it is never on the side of the superior power in such a situation. It works most effectively for the actual underdog, in this case the Soviet Union. Time, to the extent that we do not use it in furthering our own cause and perfecting our own strengths, buys for the enemy the needed days, months, and years in which to catch up and eventually, if unimpeded, surpass us. Time today not only buys the Soviet opportunity to perfect new missiles and nuclear warheads, but it also buys opportunity to make existing missiles more and more invulnerable and, more importantly, to wage virtually unrestricted political and psychological warfare. Even though we do, as at present, produce more and more nuclear weapons, our margin of superiority will thus inevitably be narrowed. In the next few years, conceivably, we could move into the perilous phase of nuclear parity. We could, in short, move into a future where the upper end of the scale of power would be as balanced in truth as it is today in popular misconception.

With a true parity situation, this would be a far different world, full of Soviet adventures which would make today's tensions seem restful by comparison. Today, the Soviet knowledge of our actual superiority keeps them in some check, although their conviction that our will is too weak to utilize that superiority gives them ample freedom to press and chip, tug and twist the West's borders, societies, policies, and internal order.

By following the underdog strategy that has inhibited us so far, America may be committing the worst strategic oversight in her history, an oversight that is more than military. In the moral and civilizational crisis in which we are involved, the sheer awe of nuclear power has led many Americans, and their elected and appointed officials, to forget the human values of the conditions of life and to become obsessed by the purely animal values of survival. Against the background of this obsession has grown the misconception that the United States and the Soviet Union are stalemated, that nuclear parity has already arrived. About the concept of stalemate there even appears to be something historically comforting. Dr. Charles Malik, whom I quoted earlier, interestingly points this out:

When some Western thinkers and leaders urge realism and accommodation, when they poke fun at the slogan of "total victory", when they manifest obvious resistance to the thought that the cold war must be fought to a successful conclusion, one is not sure that they do not thereby mean that the West must keep on losing and the realm of freedom must keep on contracting. What then are their proposals for turning the tide? I am certain they do not want to see the West overwhelmed, but some of them, I feel, do not at heart want to see Communism overwhelmed either, even if you presented them with the possibility of overwhelming it. They appear to be unwilling to contemplate the possibility of erasing it from the face of the earth.*

During the Nineteenth century, it was a balance of national powers that was supposed to have preserved the peace. Today we avoid, despite the towering evidence, asking the questions that would reveal reality to us—the

*From a recent speech.

Melvin R. Laird

Mr. Tray Dunaway
4681 Duke Station
Duke University
Durham, North Carolina 27706

READER'S DIGEST ASSN., INC., 1730 RHODE ISLAND AVE., N.W. WASHINGTON, D.C. 20036

202 223 1642

MELVIN R. LAIRD

Senior Counsellor: National and International Affairs

April 19, 1976

Dear Mr. Dunaway:

I have received your letter concerning the Celebrity-
Pro-Am Golf Tournament to raise funds for Children's
Hospital.

I am enclosing an autographed copy of House Divided
which I hope will help your project.

With best wishes and kindest personal regards, I am

reality of an America whose national power is at present unchallengeable. We avoid the responsibility of using the power which is ours. Instead we cower behind the argument that a balance of nuclear deterrents can preserve the peace and make nuclear war "unthinkable". No argument more dangerous to the United States could be propounded. The military writings of the Russians are permeated through and through with evidence that nuclear war is only unthinkable in such a period as now—when the Soviet is at the short end of the odds for victory. Present deterrence is not a balance of terror, that favorite ringing phrase of the status quorators. Present deterrence rests squarely on present American superiority.

On the day that the Soviet Union feels there is, indeed, a balance of power, it will move forward aggressively at multiples of her current pace. On that day, nuclear war will become not only thinkable but in all likelihood inevitable. On that day we will not be losing the so-called cold war; we will have lost it. Hot wars will lie ahead, or negotiated surrender to Soviet expansion.

Just as our superiority today gives us, in a realistic view, the shield behind which to press the cause of freedom, Soviet superiority or even parity tomorrow would give them the ultimate shield behind which to press the cause of the world's communization. We can rest assured that the Communists, given such a shield, would not look upon nuclear war as suicidal or as an exercise in blind mass destruction. They would look upon it first as a deterrent to Western action, and then as a means to advance Communism, and finally as the way of opening the last stage in destruction of freedom—military occupation of the United States.

It is true, as critics of my position will hasten to point

out, that Nikita Khrushchev, at the Twentieth Congress of the Communist Party, spoke of rejecting the "inevitability of war" to which Lenin and Stalin often had alluded. Lenin thought that war was inevitable so long as capitalism existed. Stalin, in his last book, wrote in 1953: "To end the inevitability of wars, it is necessary to destroy imperialism."

Khrushchev in maintaining that war was no longer inevitable, was obviously influenced by two factors: first, American superiority in any thermonuclear war; second, the success of Communist designs without resort to war. It would be dangerous indeed to conclude that, if either of these two conditions changed, Khrushchev's attitude would not change too. If the success of Communism, or the stability of the regime became threatened, the Communist leaders would resort to a war as soon as there was any chance of success; that is, as soon as actual nuclear parity was approached. It would not be regarded as an ideal situation, but if they felt they were *in extremis,* they would seize upon atomic chaos as the midwife for the salvation and ultimate victory of Communism. The greater the superiority of our military strength, however, the less likely it remains that they would do this. Taking chances is not a Communist trait. Far more probable is the development of a situation in which the Communists would resort to war as the time arrives in which they feel sure they can have overwhelming odds on their side, especially if their war-winning potential reaches a point where they become convinced we might accept an ultimatum after a few preliminary strokes, and without war's full ultimate expenditure in risk and blood. Although at present we hold a vast nuclear superiority, we must recognize that a failure of leadership in the research and development fields, and a failure to produce a winning strategy, could in three or four years reverse the present position of the United States and the Soviet Union.

This caveat demands a hard-headed consideration of the requisites for a successful strategy for the 1960's. First, such strategy must aim at deterrence, not just deterrence of war, but deterrence of the spread of Communism. Secondly, if deterrence fails, the strategy must aim at fighting, winning, and recovering. Winning means bringing the enemy's will into submission to ours. Recovery means the economic and political continuance of our national life. Each move in the strategy must be timely. Obviously it would be ridiculous to try to fight World War III with the tactics of World War II, and it would be disastrous to employ a strategy in 1962 which was appropriate for 1958 when weapons and technology were different. Finally, all elements of national policy must contribute to the over-all strategic objective—the preservation of the values discussed in the preceding chapters.

Deterrence involves communication of intent. Deterrence of an enemy move depends upon the enemy's estimation of risk, on his belief that the move may escalate to a cost level that will outweigh the intended gain. Hence, if the enemy is convinced that we will under no circumstances escalate or broaden the conflict, we reduce the risk for him, we reduce the deterrent effect, and we vastly increase the possibility of war. For, plainly, deterrence is not dependent on what will happen, but on what the enemy thinks will happen. The Berlin crisis of 1961 grew dangerously hot because President Kennedy had not made it clear that, in response to a conventional attack on West Berlin or Europe, we would respond, not on the level of war with conventional weapons, but would escalate or enlarge the struggle to a nuclear level. A speech by Senator Margaret Chase Smith, on the floor of the Senate, first produced the statement by the President that we would if necessary use nuclear weapons in defense of Berlin. The turning point in the crisis came in the period following this statement. If such a warning had been issued earlier, when President Kennedy left the Vienna conference, the Berlin crisis would never have become so serious, and it would not have been deemed necessary to call up units of the reserves and National Guard. The new President had in fact invited the Soviet's Berlin probe of his intentions; during his campaign for election he had been critical of the nuclear strategy of deterrence which alone could secure continuation of peace.

From that same background, also, came one of the most dramatic incentives for continuation of the fatal strategy of the underdog. During the latter years of the Eisenhower Administration, a new phrase was coined, the "missile gap," that gave rise to the impression that President Eisenhower had allowed the nation to become weak before its enemies. Actually the "gap" was not one of missiles; it was one of statistics. The damning figures employed to support the phrase "missile gap," resulted from Air Force estimates of what the Soviet Union *possibly* could produce *a few years after* the estimate's date. The estimate, however, was widely used in speeches by Senator John Kennedy and Senator Stuart Symington. Actually, in this time of the much touted "missile gap," 1958-1960, the Russians had developed only a handful of highly vulnerable liquid-fuel missiles. Such missiles require about a half hour for flight preparation because their highly unstable fuel cannot be kept ready in the missile itself. Sites for such missiles are, furthermore, difficult to "harden" and are thus more vulnerable to attack.

Obviously, therefore, although it was theoretically possible for the Soviets to produce such missiles on a large scale, it was extremely unlikely that they would. Such missiles would have clogged production lines with military hardware clearly headed for obsolescence. The missiles would have presented sitting duck targets for the more sophisticated missiles, the Atlas, Titan, and Polaris, then being developed in the United States. Nevertheless, Secretary of Defense Thomas Gates was loudly criticized when he told our committee that the joint intelligence community estimates disputed the "gap" statistics. The estimates of a future missile gap used by Senators Kennedy and Symington differed widely from views of the joint military intelligence community, whose own estimates were lower and of *probable* production, not *possible* production. Heat of the controversy clouded the issue and the public never understood the truth of the matter. The people remained under the misapprehension that the entire discussion was about *present* Soviet capabilities rather than about projections of its *future* capabilities.

Even today, the projection of Soviet capabilities in Air Force estimates are consistently higher than those of the joint intelligence community because of this highly significant difference in approach. Such estimates could, for example, lead to the conclusion that by 1967 there could be a missile gap, but the foreboding has nothing to do with *today's* situation. There is no dispute within the intelligence community over today's Russian capabilities. They are inferior to our own.

Although it is a conditioned reflex of the times to worry about any Soviet missiles—no matter their quantity or quality, so deeply are we imbued with the underdog complex that we are either weaker militarily or about to become weaker than the Soviet Union—there is no realistic basis for such concern. Current Soviet strike missiles are still of the vulnerable liquid-fuel variety. The Soviets are spending very little money even to attempt hardening of missile sites. Cause for concern lies more in the probable reason for their skimpy production of missiles. They seem to be awaiting a technological or espionage breakthrough that will permit development of second and third generation missiles such as Minuteman and the upgraded Polaris currently rolling off the production lines in this country. If such a breakthrough took place, then our "possible" production estimates could show grave menace indeed. But the actual situation today is that the present quantity of Russian missiles is a much lesser threat than popularly believed, precisely because it is more than balanced by a four-to-one nuclear superiority of the West. Massive production of missiles is, therefore, simply not a realistic course for the Soviet Union to follow at this time. If they get their breakthrough, however, it would be completely realistic for them to go into high gear production. Our long delay in testing our own nuclear warheads in actual missile systems made the possibility of such a breakthrough even more critical by reducing the possibility of our advances.

In the larger terms of the problem, the deterrence that prevents World War has two components. The *territorial component* is in deterring the enemy from territorial conquest. This aspect is illustrated by the military defense of Western Europe and the deterrence involved. The *psychological component* is the deterrence provided by a generally aggressive attitude. Such deterrence is immediately sapped if the enemy becomes convinced that we do not have the will to stand firm. Able use of the psychological deterrent is typically exemplified by President Eisenhower's handling of the Quemoy-Matsu crisis, where the territory itself was entirely secondary to the enemy's wish to probe the strength of our will. In a radio-television speech, President Eisenhower very cogently grasped the situation when he said:

If the Chinese Communists have decided to risk a war, it is not because Quemoy is so valuable to them. They have been getting along without Quemoy ever since they seized the China mainland nine years ago.

If they have now decided to risk a war, it can only be because they, and their Soviet allies, have decided to find out whether threatening war is a policy from which they can make big gains.

If that is their decision, then a Western Pacific Munich would not buy us peace or security. It would encourage the aggressors. It would dismay our friends and allies there. If history teaches anything, appeasement would make it more likely that we would have to fight a major war.

The Berlin crisis is an even better illustration of the psychological component in deterrence. Khrushchev wants West Berlin. But that piece of ground is of far less importance* than his aim to use Berlin to win a

---

*As Professor Stefan Possony has pointed out.

moral ascendancy over the West, seal the fate of the captive nations by having us ratify the status quo, and work toward weakening the NATO alliance by convincing the West Germans that we do not have the ability to stand firm.

Credibility to the enemy of our psychological deterrent depends, then, upon his estimation of the certainty of our response. If he believes our response will be immediate, unflinching, and single, the credibility of the response taking place is one hundred per cent. However, the percentage of the credibility diminishes with each rise of a possible weaker alternative. If it appears we may take any one of several modified courses of action, credibility diminishes with the introduction of each weaker alternate. The greater the incidence of weaker choices, the less the incidence of credibility.

During the 1961 Berlin crisis, for example, the credibility of our response was weakened by discussion over "the pause." According to the theory of "the pause", if the Communists attack, the West should, for a time, fight a conventional war in Europe. They should use this time to try to negotiate with Khrushchev. Thus, it was felt, all-out nuclear war could be avoided. That the theory of pause was being considered by some became apparent on February 27, 1961, in a story in the Washington *Evening Star,* based on a memorandum from Secretary of State Rusk to Secretary of Defense McNamara. The memorandum suggested that even massive attacks on Europe should be met with the weaker response of conventional weapons instead of nuclear weapons. The story read: "After making the enemy pause, we would point out to him the great risk in continuing his aggression, and then we would offer him a chance to negotiate." The following day Secretary Rusk called the memorandum entirely inaccurate. Nevertheless, on the heels of the Berlin crisis, publication of such thinking could not have a salutary effect. These and other reports indicated that in some high Administration quarters, persons were arguing for alternative weaker strategies, that our national policies were in a state of confusion, and that in a crisis we might not have the decision-making capabilities to act unequivocally.* After that, a Berlin probe became inevitable.

Actually, the Berlin problem had not changed since 1953 when during a visit I was briefed on it as an area of psychological warfare by General Norstad. General Norstad also used the term "pause" in 1959. During the Eisenhower Administration, however, the word appeared in an entirely different context. Norstad's position, as stated in his testimony on the "Mutual Security Act of 1959", was that ". . . we must force a conscious decision on the part of the Russians that they either will or will not go to war. They can't slide into it, they can't back into it, they can't wake up some morning and find they have gone too far." This was a proper strategic attitude. The NATO shield had to be strong enough so that the Soviets could not conduct probing actions. Before the Conference of the NATO parliamentarians November 21, 1960, Norstad said:

The forces which are assigned to the NATO mission require the support of nuclear weapons. The defense of Europe against a serious large-scale attack, certainly depends on these weapons. . . .

---

*The Cuban debacle is a notable illustration of what can actually happen, when strategic requirements have not been clarified at the highest levels.

The forces of Allied Command Europe must be organized, equipped, trained and deployed so as to be able to react promptly and effectively with:

First, conventional weapons, when such weapons are adequate to the military situation.

Second, atomic weapons, when the use of such weapons is necessary.

Except in certain well-defined cases of direct self-defense, atomic weapons should be introduced into battle only after a particular decision to do so has resulted from the operation of an established decision-making process. This process will ensure that such a decision would, in all cases, be taken by an authority at a level higher than that of the basic combat unit, and that the level of combat would have been raised above that which could be dealt with by conventional weapons.

A great English newspaper, while it was recently exercising what has become the general privilege and practice of criticising NATO policies, stated that SACEUR believes "that any penetration of the land frontiers ought to be stopped decisively, at once, if necessary, by the use of nuclear weapons." This, I wish to say, is exactly what I believe.

These quotations indicate the position of the Eisenhower Administration and illustrate Norstad's notable success with the Berlin problem. Especially in the missile age, when missiles in flight, unlike bombers, cannot be called back, the NATO shield must force a real decision on the part of an aggressor. On the other hand, an idea of pausing to fight the enemy first with conventional weapons, without any threat of intercession with our nuclear superiority, undermines deterrence by presenting the alternative of the weaker response. It makes perilous probing highly probable, because it allows the enemy to specify the rules of the contest.

In the Korean War, under the Truman Administration, we chose to permit the enemy to set the ground rules of the contest. How was the Korean War finally ended? When the Chinese Communists did not join in a truce, the United States warned she would bomb north of the Yalu, might blockade the Chinese coast, might use tactical atomic weapons, and would aim at winning a united Korea. This was a strong response on a rising scale, essentially the same as the earlier strategy recommended by MacArthur, and rejected by President Truman. The Eisenhower Administration's new policies meant that, for the Red Chinese, ascending risk was again injected into the war, risk that the war might be expanded on definitely named, increasingly disadvantageous terms to the Red Chinese. We would no longer allow the Red Chinese to fight from a privileged sanctuary. All of this information, in principle, was conveyed through Prime Minister Nehru to the Chinese Communists. It was this strategy which produced the truce, and its success formed the basis for the Eisenhower-Dulles policy. Dulles notified the Communists that in any future aggression over Korea, the aggressor would not be permitted to set forth favorable ground rules for his aggression.

The policies of definite deterrence were further explained by Secretary Dulles before the Council of Foreign Relations on January 12, 1954. A basic decision had been made, the Secretary said, "to depend primarily upon a great capacity to retaliate instantly by means and at places of our choosing." Plainly, Dulles was seeking ways to gain freedom of action and to avoid Korean-type wars where the enemy was permitted to set the ground rules.

Dulles' strategy, however, was misinterpreted to mean that we would respond to all levels of aggression by all-out atomic bombing of Russia and Red China. At press conferences in March, 1954, the Secretary pointed out that he had in no place said the United States would necessarily retaliate instantly. He was, however, seeking ways to avoid the policy of simple containment that allows the enemy the initiative. The possibility that we might strike at the privileged sanctuary of the Red Chinese in Manchuria was and is an idea quite different from a response of dropping bombs on Peking or Moscow. Mr. Dulles also explained:

... a would-be aggressor will hesitate to commit aggression if he knows in advance that he thereby not only exposes these particular forces which he chooses to use for his aggression, but also deprives his other assets of "sanctuary" status. That does not mean that if there is a Communist attack somewhere in Asia, atom or hydrogen bombs will necessarily be dropped on the great industries of China or Russia.

At many other times in his career Dulles took pains to point out that this strategy was not what most critics meant in referring to "massive retaliation." Dulles envisioned a selective range of actions at times and places of our own choosing. On July 18, 1956, Dulles emphasized that our defensive policy was expressed in terms of primary reliance upon selective deterrent power. In the 1956 State of the Union message President Eisenhower called for "an effective flexible type of power calculated to deter or repulse aggression and to preserve the peace." In an article appearing on April 21, 1955, Hanson Baldwin stated that a strategy of measured retaliation was being discussed in regard to possible Chinese Communist aggression. The strategy encompassed response to such aggression through the initial destruction of, perhaps, one Communist airfield on the mainland. This nuclear strike would be a credible warning. If the aggression continued, intensifying reprisals could be taken.

The key element in the deterrence equation is the calculus of risk. During the Eisenhower Administration there had been many advocates of limited war in the sense that both opponents would agree to some ceiling on the level of violence. In effect, this was the Korean-type war. Dulles was not against keeping the level of violence limited, if we controlled the initiative of setting the limitation. As he said as early as November 28, 1954:

The essential thing is that we and our Allies should have the means and the will to assure that a potential aggressor would lose from his aggression more than he could win. This does not mean that the aggressor has to be totally destroyed. It does mean a capacity to inflict punishing damage.

Plainly, he who has the power to control escalation has the power of initiative, the power to control war and peace.

What Dulles was unwilling to do was to permit the Communists to set the time, place, and weapons of the contest to their advantage. When that is permitted, the element of risk is taken out of deterrence, and deterrence fails.

In 1961, however, talk of limited war in the sense of both powers agreeing to some ceiling of violence had weakened deterrence, and the weakening contributed to the Berlin crisis. Fortunately, as the Berlin crisis deepened there were statements which showed better recognition of deterrent policy. The most significant of these was by Assistant Secretary of Defense Paul Nitze.

Warnings, however, should not always be too specific as to their precise nature. It is often best to be somewhat ambiguous about the means that we would use, particularly the final means. If we reveal fully our strategy and tactics, it will enable the enemy to adjust to the circumstance, and present a challenge a little bit different from what we estimated and had stated. On the other hand, it is very important to be specific in regard to the fact that we *will* act in defense of vital interests, or in defense of certain territory and that action will be swift and decisively unpleasant for the enemy. President Kennedy's earlier statements on Laos gravely weakened the credibility of his later statements. Only disastrous consequences can result from making threats and then failing to back them up, indicating first a strong course of action and then retreating to a weaker one. The man who waves a big stick while a situation is developing, and then at the moment of necessary action emerges with a twig, will not retain the respect of his neighbors in such a way as to make them careful how they offend him in the future. The important points to be noted are firmness of initial decision and the application of alternatives which shall be in ascending forcefulness instead of representing a sliding away to weakness. This does not mean that at the same time the enemy may not be left in doubt as to the exact weapons that will be applied. He should be in no doubt at all, however, that application is forthcoming, nor should he ever be given the satisfying experience of being able to prove to himself and to the watching world that threats made against him were not in earnest, or that action has not been as strong as the promises of action. What would have been appropriate, and is appropriate in Vietnam, for example, is to warn decisively and with absolute inner firmness of resolution that we will defend Vietnam's vital interests if necessary and if called upon, but not to state the exact means that will be used in such defense. The aim is to keep the enemy guessing about weapons and methods, but to leave him with the steady certainty that we will act, and that the action will be effective. After all, it was leaving the North Koreans with the certainty that we would *not* act that led to the Korean war.

Today more than at any other period in history, war— not peace—could become the wages of the weak.

5

IF DETERRENCE FAILS

IF DETERRENCE FAILS, we must have the capability both
to fight and win a war. Wars are waged with military
forces. The most effective strategy aims at the defeat of
the enemy's armed might. As Chief of Staff of the Air
Force, General Curtis Le May has written, "Only defeat
of *military* forces can win a war and only a force that is
clearly able to defeat an aggressor's military force is
likely to deter war. We believe that we can deter armed
aggression by being able to fight and win any war that is
forced upon us—including a general war."*

Our strategic policies and all our research and development must aim at the capability, not of fighting to a
stalemate, but of defeating the aggressor. It greatly
weakens our strategic posture each time we talk about
devising a nuclear strategy aiming simply at negotiation
or bargaining. All warfare is based upon deception,
said the ancient Chinese sage, Sun Tzu. It would be an
invitation to disaster if either China or Russia believed
that we might pause to negotiate after a nuclear strike.

There was discussion some years ago of a strategy of
minimum deterrence which would aim at deterring war
merely by the destruction of certain Russian cities. The

---

*See *Army Reservist Magazine,* Jan., 1962.

strategy did not present a concept of victory, but merely of punishment. Even if such strategy might have seemed applicable at a time when Russia had little if any real nuclear capability, it is no longer possible when she possesses a range of effective nuclear weapons. We must have the will and the capacity to fight and win decisively. At the same time, civil defense becomes important. The eventuality of nuclear war must not leave us so prostrate that our republic cannot continue.

All strategic requisities must be coordinated by the aim of preserving our way of life. We will not possess a rational strategy if it leads into duplicating the irrational mistakes of World War I and World War II, where we had no long-range goals. In each case, our soldiers won the war and our leaders lost the peace, and our lack of coherent, long-range, abiding strategy prepared the next conflict.

Since World War II, we have been involved in a series of swiftly changing strategy phases. The first, or the monopoly phase, was one where we alone possessed nuclear power; the Soviets had none. With our nuclear monopoly, we had punishment capacity in our nuclear weapons, and this was a period when the strategy of the minimum deterrent was actually applicable. We deterred Soviet invasion of Europe by the threat of selective atomic retaliation at times and places of our own choosing. For lesser Soviet threats we had more limited measures at hand, both nuclear and conventional. Not all punishments would be nuclear, but would fit the crime. Meanwhile, the Soviet Union could not retaliate. Of the effectiveness of this imbalance and the developments it prevented, there can be little doubt. As Winston Churchill said on March 31, 1949, in summarizing the nature of the monopoly phase, "It is certain that Europe would have been communized and London under bombardment some time ago but for the deterrent of the atomic bomb in the hands of the United States."

However, the deterrent which was adequate for the monopoly phase was not at all adequate in the period that followed. This second phase may be called the phase of our "European continental superiority." In this time of transition, the United States still had, in any action in Western Europe, a vast nuclear preponderance. Despite Soviet Russia's acquisition of the atomic secret, she did not have long-range bombers capable of carrying the bomb to the United States, while we had the aircraft and the rings of bases needed to reach her territory. But even during this second phase, a minimum deterrent strategy was still adequate. In any all-out war, the United States would still have nuclear superiority, and practically speaking, nuclear war as an instrument in the advance of Communism was impossible in the cold hard light of Soviet realism as to means. Escalation was to her disadvantage for, at the top of the stairway of violence, we retained our devastating superiority. The twilight of Phase Two came sometime in 1957 or 1958 when the Soviets developed their large numbers of intermediate range missiles to meet our nuclear capability in Western Europe.

The next phase, or Phase Three, could be called the phase of "heartland superiority" of the United States over Soviet Russia. Conceivably, the Soviet Union might devise a strategy whereby she would strike with nuclear weapons at Western Europe, present the United States with a fait accompli, and then offer a chance for a negotiated settlement which it would be presumed the United States would accept to avoid all-out nuclear war. Such a stroke was unlikely, but no longer totally unrealistic. But still unrealistic, in the face of the cool clearheadedness typical of Soviet military thinking, was initiation of nuclear war in which it was certain that the United States would retaliate in our superior kind.

During the latter part of this phase, however, the Soviet Union obtained a capability to attack the continental United States; the American heartland itself became vulnerable to atom bombs and intercontinental ballistic missiles. The Soviets had advanced from the capability of holding Western Europe hostage, to a capability of holding, not our whole country, but a sizable number of key cities similarly as "hostages." These conditions, however—threatening though they soon became —were still not those of nuclear parity, because the United States continued to possess a strong margin of nuclear dominance even in a second strike, and an overwhelming dominance in a first strike. We are currently still in Phase Three. Our goal now must be to prohibit development of the subsequent phase aimed at by the Soviets—actual nuclear parity, or worse yet, Soviet nuclear superiority.

As already noted, beginning in 1958, many persons were saying that the Soviets already possessed nuclear parity. In a Senate speech on August 14, 1958, then Senator Kennedy expressed his alarm about the missile gap, and called upon the United States to follow an "underdog strategy." Similarly, in June 1960, Governor Rockefeller released a statement in which he indicated his alarm over Soviet missile superiority. The very able writer-professor, Henry Kissinger, likewise based many of his observations in his excellent book, *Nuclear Weapons and Foreign Policy*, on the assumption that we were caught in a missile gap. Each of these observers mistakenly assumed that we had moved into the fourth strategic stage, that our nuclear preponderance was lost, and that deterrence by nuclear power was only a frail hope. These assumptions led then Senator Kennedy to advocate his "underdog" strategy. It was thus that we entered the full swing of our extremely damaging "underdog" strategy.

The strategy was baseless—a fact difficult to find a hearing for at first, but now almost universally acknowledged. One of the most outspoken men on the subject of our present superiority is Deputy Defense Secretary Roswell Gilpatric. Speaking in Hot Springs, Virginia, on October 21, 1961, Gilpatric said, "The United States has today hundreds of manned intercontinental bombers capable of reaching the Soviet Union, including six hundred heavy bombers and many more medium bombers equally capable of intercontinental operations ... (the United States) also has six Polaris submarines at sea carrying a total of ninety-six missiles, and dozens of intercontinental ballistic missiles. Our carrier strike forces and land based ... forces could deliver additional hundreds of megatons. The total number of our nuclear delivery vehicles, tactical as well as strategic, is in the tens of thousands; and of course, we have more than one warhead for each vehicle ... Therefore, we are confident that the Soviets will not provoke a major nuclear conflict." Gilpatric said that such a move "would be an act of self-destruction on his part." Yet, it does us little good to have this superiority if we actually follow what looks like an "underdog" strategy.

At present the new and fourth phase *will* occur if the United States and the Soviet Union begin to approach *real nuclear parity*. Even though one side still had a slight edge over the other, there would then exist two invulnerable retaliatory forces, and each nation would have, after being hit first by the other, enough strike-back to deliver massive and unacceptable damage. It is in this final development of Phase Four that we would actually lose our nuclear advantage. In its closing period it would be a stage which for the West would make nuclear war realistically impossible. The final portions of Phase Four would create a situation in which we would become incapable of winning *militarily*, since both sides would have hardened, invulnerable missile systems and an "overkill" capacity as well. But *politically*, there would arise a deadly modification of so called parity. We could not win but, conceivably, the Communists could. Even if Russia were destroyed, or Red China lost, Communism still could advance from its other bases.

Many options would then be open to the Communists. Suppose the end of Phase Four did come into actual being some years hence. Red China, backed by its own ICBM's could launch a massive land attack into South Korea, South Vietnam, Cambodia, Burma, and Thailand, while at the same time Soviet Russia, poised with nuclear weapons, would do nothing. What could be our counterstroke? Should we go all-out in nuclear retaliation? If so, what sort of targets would Red China offer? And how would we react if, after some limited American nuclear strikes, the Soviet Union announced she would become the mediator in the war between Red China and the United States and that, in the face of this mediation, either nation that continued to resort to any use of nuclear weapons might suffer additional nuclear consequences from "peace-loving" Soviet Russia? As we went to the conference table, ostensibly designed to preserve restraint from nuclear weapons in our time, the Red Chinese conquest could be consolidated with conventional forces, and Red China would dominate all Southeast Asia. World Communism would then have the Free World surrounded indeed, and Stalin's prediction of our encirclement would have found its fatal fulfillment.

Or take another example. Suppose the Soviet Union developed a space platform and, with the usual massive exploitation characteristic of its propaganda, announced its position in relation to the Unied States—rotating in space over us, and loaded with a super bomb of more than one hundred megatons? Then suppose there had developed in West Germany a pro-Communist minority demanding unification. Finally, suppose Khrushchev or his successor announced that NATO now threatened not only the peaceful unification of Germany, but the peace of the world; that West Germany must lay down its arms and abandon NATO; that if this was not done within two weeks, Soviet Russia would have no recourse but to conduct a "disarming attack"; that surely the United States would not want to interfere with these Soviet peace measures and cause the Soviet Union to bring into play its weapon on the space platform?

In estimating such dread eventualities, the average citizen is apt to think that the Pentagon has some sort of magic that can select the appropriate counter-strategies—using mechanical computors, mathematicians, or some other scientific approach developed by the engineers of our complex society. It is true that these means are important. The Pentagon's use of statistics and its mechanical devices for war-gaming are indispensable. But we create conditions for disaster when mechanical means are allowed to determine future strategy.* In the Vinson-McNamara RS-70 controversy, overvaluation of the computors as strategists became the issue, the occasion for alarm, rather than the realistic programming of the RS-70 itself. It was said that the RS-70 had been "computed out of existence." Computers can work only with the information they are fed, and supplying us with credible misinformation is a Russian specialty. The Communists can throw the computers off—as easily as they threw off our intelligence reports on bomber production after 1955—as easily as they fooled us about missile production after 1958. The Chinese sage, Sun Tzu, was right when he said that warfare is based on deception, and nothing is more vulnerable to deception than the unimaginative computor. In the dozen years ahead, the Communists will maximize deception. At the very time when we think they are going all out on building surface-to-surface missiles, they in fact may be going all out in research on weapons for outer space— where the decisive battles may well be fought. Surprise is not the exception in war; it is the rule. The building of the Berlin wall caught our government totally by surprise, as did the resumption of Soviet nuclear testing.

Computor-mindedness is intensely dangerous. It can not give us all the answers about future military uses of space. What is more, in actuality, key decisions are

---

*Although, as a member of the Defense Appropriations Subcommittee I sided with McNamara on funding the RS-70 in fiscal 1963, my decision was based on entirely different premises.

made in an atmosphere of swiftly changing crisis. If we have not developed steady policy or coherent over-all goals as guides, crisis will catch us without any policy at all, and inevitably we will fall into lethal errors. There was a swiftly changing crisis when the air support of the Cuban invasion was called off, and the Communists—instructed by observing our confusion—will create future crises in which our leaders will be forced to make sudden decisions. Very worrying is a recent statement by Defense Secretary McNamara, who declared, "Our new policy gives us the flexibility to choose among several operational plans, but does not require that we make any advance commitment with respect to *doctrine or targets*." (Emphasis supplied) Is it really conceivable that we make no commitment to doctrine or targets? Earlier in this statment, the Defense Secretary had said, "We may seek to terminate a war on favorable terms by using our forces as a bargaining weapon—by threatening further attack." Is there not implication here of the fatal concept of the "pause to negotiate," applied this time to all-out nuclear world war?

Limited use of nuclear weapons will have a very important role to play in the future, but let us not endanger our perilous but still tenable Phase Three by acting without doctrine and without strategy! Our doctrine and our strategy must provide for the Communist nature, for maximum surprise, and for the unexpected. The most dangerous situation conceivable would be to leave all questions to the hour of crisis, when a group of Presidential advisers, perhaps beguiled by a Communist trap, would hover around the President, and seek to influence him. Only doctrine—firm and carefully reasoned in advance—can prevent such an eventuality.

The objective of our present strategy must be to

prohibit Phase Four in its entirety. We must retain and *increase* our superiority, not lose it. We must have the ability to *win,* not merely to punish. And in moving toward this goal, we must have a steadily accurate estimation of which stage we are currently in. Such estimates become the proper foundation of doctrine, as doctrine is the proper foundation of diplomacy. Since we have superiority and have not incorporated it into our diplomacy, we are losing an essential advantage in our contest with Communism.

The Soviet Union is currently waging a war throughout the entire spectrum of power. An essential key to their strategy is nuclear blackmail. The only way we can defeat its effectiveness is by incorporating in our diplomacy our own superior nuclear capability. In other words, their nuclear blackmail is a bluff. We must call their bluff, now, while we can—or deterrence will indeed fail and so will the West.

The Soviet strategy of nuclear blackmail is geared to maintaining pressure just short of all-out war. It is based upon a willingness to go a little closer to the brink of war than we will. Actually, the Soviet Union is unwilling to take a real risk of war, as long as we hold our nuclear lead. But they maintain the advantage when, in Phase Three, although we still hold an edge in nuclear power, we succumb to the underdog strategy and behave as if we were in Phase Four, when the Soviets are assumed to have parity, or even—as some hysterical statements held in 1960-61—an actual superiority. The so-called "underdog strategy" was not only false, but everything stemming from it has tended to national suicide. While there is still time to correct the tragic error, the underdog strategy must give way to a strategy of initiative.

PART II
Elements of a Public Strategy

6

THE STRATEGY OF INITIATIVE

THE UNDERDOG STRATEGY, with its abdication of moral responsibility and its suicidal preference for running rather than risking, depends by its own admission on the good will of the Communist leaders. This type of naiveté is precisely as fatal now as it was in 1938 when men depended on the good will of Adolf Hitler. Peace in our time was the slogan then, and nations in its name sacrificed conscience for the sake of peace, while the dictators grew strong on the shattered freedoms of helpless peoples. The end is known to all; we lost both conscience and the peace, and prepared the way for this new time, the same horror on a deeper level.

One may ask how often history must teach such a lesson before it is finally learned. To keep the peace today and tomorrow depends upon asserting the consciences of free men. It depends on seizing the initiative instead of running away. It depends on courage, on honesty, on the sense of ultimate values which gave America her growth and now makes her the fulcrum of the Free World. And it depends most immediately on finding the willingness to act without equivocation, announcing publicly and in such a manner as to leave no doubt, that the United States will take the initiative, not hesitating to strike first if the Communist Empire further moves to threaten the peace of the world, or the freedom of other peoples.

Making it credible to the enemy that we will take the initiative and strike first if necessary does not follow the pattern of a so-called preventive war; it does not mean constructing a subterranean plot to launch an attack against the Soviet Union whenever such attack is practical. What it means is serving credible notice, and meaning it, that we reserve to ourselves the initiative to strike first when the Soviet peril point rises beyond its tolerable limit. The tolerable limit would not, of course, be too tightly defined lest the Russians use it—as they have used our many "defense perimeter" statements—merely as a guide as to how far they may goad us with impunity.

Credible announcement of first strike initiative is the sole way to effective disarmament discussions with the Soviet Union. So long as the leaders of the Communist Empire are assured that we will never take the initiative, but will always remain on the defensive, there is no conceivable reason for them to agree to serious arms controls or the inspection systems upon which such controls must be based, if they are to be effective.

A secondary, but extremely valuable, effect of first strike initiative would be that it would force the Soviet Union to divert more of its war efforts and budget to the building of defenses rather than aggressive weapons. It would be a significant step toward our control of situations, the type of control in which we have been so notably weak in the past.

Even sympathetic critics may ask if such an announcement of first strike initiative is really necessary—whether it might be better just to let the Communists guess our intentions, leaving them an even broader area of doubt? The difficulty is that since March 28, 1961, it cannot for a moment be supposed the Communists are in any doubt whatever about the limited area of our intentions. On that date, President Kennedy in a message to Congress, said that "our arms will never be used to strike the first blow in any attack."

Despite the open statement, Western analysts sought the reassurance of second guessing, of saying that the President, in effect, either didn't mean what he said or later changed his mind. They were swiftly disillusioned. When Stewart Alsop, in the *Saturday Evening Post* on March 31, 1962 said that President Kennedy had indeed effected a major change in national policy—to the effect that we would strike first, the White House issued a prompt correction—not only for Americans, but for the carefully listening Communist generals. Press Secretary Pierre Salinger expressed the Administration's intentions in unmistakable terms:

It has always been clear that in such a context as a massive conventional attack on Europe by the Soviet Union, which would put Europe in danger of being overrun, the West would have to *prevent* such an event by all available means. This has been United States policy since the late Nineteen Forties and it represents *no change*.

Our committee in Congress took a different position. In the report on the Defense Appropriations Bill for 1961, we went further than saying that all means including nuclear weapons should be used in case a massive attack began and was in process of overrunning Europe.

We said, in effect, we should be willing to take the initiative:

In the final analysis, to effectively deter a would-be aggressor, we should maintain our armed forces in such a way and with such an understanding that should it ever become obvious that an attack upon us or our allies is imminent, we can launch an attack *before the aggressor has hit* either us or our allies. This is an element of deterrence which the United States should not deny itself. No other form of deterrence can be fully relied upon.

Certainly, if we continue the policy stated by President Kennedy, and if we announce it to the world by proclaiming that we will never use our power to initiate a first strike and only respond to a first attack by our enemy, we are encouraging the Russians never to be serious about over-all disarmament. We are also putting ourselves in a position that will save the Russians billions of dollars in their defense costs through eliminating the requirements for nuclear survival. The United States has been forced to harden its missile sites; the Russians have not. Conceivably, they need never harden their missile complex.

The fact is that America is caught between alternatives. Either a policy of first strike must be developed, together with its credible announcement, or the urgent measures of an actual underdog must be undertaken. These are the measures which would inevitably arise when and if we do enter into Phase Four, when Russia's nuclear strength through our own irresponsibility or some other cause closely approaches ours. We would have to develop greatly increased conventional strength. During Phase Two, after we had lost our monopoly of nuclear power, and Russia had the atom bomb (but only we had the necessary strength in bases and bombers to carry atomic destruction to the heart of the enemy), we maintained, theoretically, the ground strength needed to implement this strategy. (In actuality, however, our ground forces were inadequately modernized, and the NATO shield was not adequate to the goals set for it. The total number of allied divisions in the free world was two hundred.) Our ground strength was only sufficient in view of our strategy of massive nuclear deterrent, which presented the enemy with the risk that we might selectively retaliate, enlarge the conflict, destroy his weapons of war.

This strategy and these conventional force levels, adequate in the 1950's during Phase Two, when we were successfully following Dulles' unequivocally enunciated policy of selective retaliation, are totally inadequate for the 1960's. In the 1960's, for bitter reasons which may involve our own negligence, we may face Soviet achievement of real nuclear parity. Once such parity is reached, the Communist powers will possess a new freedom of action to commit aggression on the conventional level. If the Administration continues to encourage the development of Phase Four by conducting its diplomacy as if we were already in it, our plans to meet the inevitable Russian conventional attacks with conventional forces at best approximately equal to those we had during Phase Two, will leave us without hope of survival. In Phase Two our conventional forces were adequate only because we could back them with the deterrent threat of our nuclear advantage. In Phase Four the nuclear advantage will have passed to the Soviets. Thus the course which the present Administration has chosen places us in an extremely dangerous position. What it represents is dominance of the irrationality which now holds sway over too many national leaders.

To reestablish a dialogue on strategy within our nation, it is necessary to face facts as they are, and to debate whether we really are willing to take the initiative to preserve freedom. Step One of a military strategy of initiative should be the credible announcement of our determination to strike first if necessary to protect our vital interests. Step Two should be to explore the use of limited nuclear reprisals, to learn how this can be combined with coherent diplomacy, and to discover how our policies should be communicated to the enemy to further increase our powers of deterrence in an age when both sides will be hardening their missiles.

It is obvious that willingness to undertake nuclear reprisals will be imperative if we enter the initial part of Phase Four where the United States and the Soviet Union each have a devastating strikeback capability. Then Russia might be tempted to seize West Berlin and use this blow as a world symbol of the changing balance of power. But the United States could prevent this by credible notice in advance that in case of such an event it would make nuclear strikes on Soviet troop concentrations. The threat would not be to initiate all-out nuclear war, which would force the Soviet Union into all-out counter war. This would not be a rational step, nor would such a threat be believed by the Soviet Union at a time when both powers had an "overkill" capacity. But limited retaliation would be a rational step, even in an age of nuclear parity, and the Soviet realists would understand it. The key to the deterrent effect of such a strategy is the credible forewarning. Our willingness for the limited strike, plus the enemy's belief in our willingness, would mean in all probability that such a strike would never be necessary. This is a fact, but it should never delude us into thinking we are playing a game of bluff.

The strategy of threatening selective reprisal was first explored and used during the tenure in office of Secretary Dulles. For example, in 1955 there was considered a policy called "2X", according to which nuclear punishment would be dealt an aggressor at a rate estimated at twice the aggressor's potential gain. "The punishment will fit the crime, only double" as James Reston explained in his column. Hanson Baldwin called the strategy one of "measured retaliation." What it meant was that if the Red Chinese, for instance, assaulted Quemoy or Matsu, one Red Chinese airfield on the mainland would be destroyed. After this clear (and most credible!) warning, continuance of the aggression would result in the destruction of another airfield, then another, until the point at which cost to the enemy would outweigh the gain. As it would then turn out, as soon as the potential aggressor understood in advance the retaliation his aggression would trigger, he would be deterred from the aggression in the first place.

It is in the light of these experiences that a way may now be found for their larger strategic application in the 1960's. Plainly, such a strategy has to evolve from Step One of a strategy of initiative, open adoption—credible adoption—of a first strike policy when necessary. For this strategy of reprisals envisions forewarning the enemy as to our initiative, even with nuclear weapons, to make his aggression unprofitable. Obviously, a failure to adopt such a strategy can greatly lower—indeed has lowered—our deterrence capabilities. And for those who would inevitably cry out the accusation, "war-monger!" at the initial advocates of the first-strike policy, it should be pointed out—as Winston Churchill shrewdly observed—that it is the deterrent power of the United States which alone has preserved, and still preserves, the peace of the world. "War-mongers" today are not those who realistically face the furiously irrational core of aggressive Communism and, in willingness to see and understand the truth, argue the necessity for maintenance of our national strength; the actual people who court war are those who flee the facts, refuse a realistic dialogue on strategy, misunderstand the enemy, and unwittingly place America in the situation of national weakness which invites attack. It is weakness in the United States, not its strength, which may mean the war in our time.

Before leaving consideration of the policy of selective retaliation, Step Two in adopting a strategy of the initiative, it is necessary to note an important distinction. Secretary of Defense McNamara has indicated, as I quoted him earlier, that "we may seek to terminate a war on favorable terms by using our forces as a bargaining weapon—by threatening further attack." The Secretary's suggestion does not parallel my proposal; it is the opposite. The Secretary implies a pause to negotiate in a major nuclear attack—one in which we will have stood by and taken the first blow. My contention is that it is utterly fatal to indicate to the enemy at any time that we would ever entertain a bargaining proposal after he has made his all-out nuclear attack. This course is simply an invitation to him to ready his bombs and attack us. This attitude could ultimately lead to national suicide.

My suggestion is in a different context and should not

be misunderstood. It means that in cases of lesser enemy aggressions—such as seizure of Berlin, or in certain similar situational and sublimited war actions where we have profitable military targets—we should in advance clearly and credibly warn the enemy we will undertake military reprisals that obviously would outweigh the gain. He, not we, would be placed in the position of asking for bargains. Secretary McNamara's statement, I fear, indicates a lack of understanding of the Communist mind. Unfortunately, many of his recent pronouncements on our national strategy have raised a rash of questions by people of all opinions. While still maintaining we would never strike first, he indicates that our retaliation, a type of "no-city counterforce strategy" would avoid Soviet cities and hit only at Soviet military forces. While logical in a first strike strategy, which is one of the major proposals of this book, in a second strike, this seems to place us in the position of firing at empty missile sites. I hope that by the time of the publication of this book these serious contradictions will have been clarified by the President. If not, these confusions in our strategy could invite another Berlin crisis.

The third step necessary for a strategy of initiative would be to arm our NATO allies with defensive nuclear weapons, under proper controls. If West Germany and France could use defensive nuclear weapons, Khrushchev's strategy to disrupt NATO would at once suffer a major defeat. Krushchev knows this, and is making every possible effort to prevent us from extending the power of the nuclear deterrent to our allies. And the present Administration shows every indication of cooperation. President Kennedy appears unwilling to

contradict Khrushchev even by giving nuclear arms to
General de Gaulle. It is a peculiar anomaly when a great
nation refuses to its friends the military secrets already
long since stolen by their common enemy. The fact is
that Khrushchev's nuclear blackmail strategy which he
uses to terrify Europe would be shattered if we "nucle-
arized" our allies. He could no longer say to our individual and exposed allies, such as West Germany,
France, and Italy, that he could deal with them before
they could defend themselves. Our allies, while incapable of defeating Russia, could deter her most effectively if they had the power to retaliate with nuclear
weapons. That is why Khrushchev is so determined
they shall not get them. Nuclear deterrent in the hands
of the allied powers would be a great help to us. It
would provide us with a bargaining vehicle for insist-
ing, in return, that they meet their conventional force
requirements. Three Administrations—Truman's, Eisenhower's, and Kennedy's—have failed to bring NATO
up to the strength needed by a conventional shield
force. With nuclear weapons, France and Britain would
no longer have an excuse for withholding funds that
should go into their own conventional shield and putting them into nuclear development instead—development that we could give them.*

On the subject of nuclear weapons for our allies, Mal-
colm Mackintosh had an interesting article in *Army*
magazine for May, 1960, and while I do not agree with
all the points made, the theme is meaningful. Mackintosh points out that to Soviet strategists a short war

---

*Henry A. Kissinger, in "The Unsolved Problems of European De-
fense (*Foreign Affairs*, July, 1962) , makes an excellent case in an
examination of the need for European nuclear self-defense.

is a myth. Victory will go to the side that can preserve its armed forces from nuclear destruction for the longest period, and then keep them able to fight beyond the point of national exhaustion. It is interesting to place this theme beside a statement by Dr. Stefan Possony, whom we quoted earlier and who worked for several significant years with the Chief of Staff of the Air Force. "Today," said Dr. Possony, "military establishments which do not have nuclear weapons are little more than oversized gendarmeries. In a future conflict, a nuclear force will crush its non-nuclear opponents almost instantly."

In an all-out war, with our non-nuclear allies faced by Russians with nuclear arms, our allies would be absolutely incapable of stopping or even delaying the mammoth Soviet armies that would push across Europe. Even if we meanwhile rained nuclear bombs on the Soviet heartland our allies themselves would be helpless. There is much controversy as to whether the Russians now entertain the concept of this type of offensive, but the writings cited by Mackintosh indicate that some Soviet militarists have played with the idea. If the Soviets ever reach a point of considering the launching of a nuclear attack, they may again speculate on the advantages of their armies spreading across Europe, Africa, and the mid-East. The obvious and only way to end this temptation is to give our allies the proper deterrent weapons.

As was pointed out earlier, the fears played up by Soviet propaganda that such a weapons grant would allow the possibility of military adventures by, say, West Germany are unreasonable and totally without recognition of the facts. The structure of interdependence that has been built into the NATO military force and, notably, into the West German armed forces, absolutely assures the United States effective control.* It is ludicrous to assume that Germany today, segmented and sick of conflict, would engage in an offensive on her own that would lead to World War III, end her present prosperity, and unleash upon herself the most ruthless political and military machine in humanity's history.

After the proper arming of her allies, the fourth step in developing within the United States a coherent and unequivocal strategy of initiative is the adequate testing and rapid development of our own nuclear weapons. We must clearly realize our own and the world's peril, honestly facing up to our responsibilities as free men and as the vanguard of the Free World, aware of our values and unflinching in sustaining them—throwing away none of our advantages, whether in weapons testing or any other area. Here we come to the heart of the Soviet Union's cold war strategy. Much has been said about nibbling aggression and wars of liberation, about a Sino-Soviet victory through slice-by-slice "salami tactics," and it is true that until Khrushchev achieves a decisive technological superiority, this type of action will remain his great hope of success. But he also hopes to use his so-called support of "anti-colonialism" and "wars of liberation" as decoys. It must be hoped that this Administration has not been so obtuse as really to be deceived by the decoy so as to divert its attention from the underlying design of Soviet strategy. Dr. Possony very ably describes the issue:

---

*During a recent breakfast at which I entertained the German Ambassador to Washington, he clearly indicated that his country understood this and that such control of atomic weapons could be worked out.

The Cold War usually is interpreted as a propaganda contest, as economic competition, or as a series of small conflicts for the control of underdeveloped countries. This is just one "axis" of the multidimensional Cold War and by no means the most important. The Cold War, as waged by the Communists, is the sum total of all lesser conflict operations designed to make nuclear aggression feasible and profitable, or unnecessary (for the Soviets). *Its main purpose is to achieve technological superiority in all major weapon systems, notably in nuclear weapons.* (emphasis supplied)

How can anyone who really studies the problem fail to see that Possony is correct? We are now locked in a real war, joined in mortal combat on the battlefield, each contender maneuvering for advantage—as frankly as Napoleon at Waterloo or Lee at Gettysburg, only on a scale a thousand times magnified. Our own war, its battlefield and its maneuvers for advantage, is not of merely geographical dimensions as at Waterloo and Gettysburg. This is a war of technology, a battlefield of research, and maneuvers in these areas for break-throughs. The Soviets will use every trick and stratagem to beguile us into sacrificing our time and efforts to hopes of disarmament. If meanwhile they achieve their own breakthrough in advanced or space weapons, they will revise their strategy; and instead of being confronted by so-called "wars of liberation," the world will face all-out nuclear terror, a situation from which our own nuclear capability will have been eliminated.

I am seriously concerned by current strategic policies that do not see this danger, and are not placing maximum emphasis on testing. That we now possess an overwhelming superiority of nuclear delivery vehicles *cannot protect us from technological breakthroughs!* We

must work and move ahead ceaselessly. We must understand the Soviet strategy for what it is, and realize that
the technological battleground is a decisive arena of the
Cold War. Meanwhile, we must use every advantage we
possess by integrating into our diplomacy the facts of
our present superiority. This is the fifth necessary step
in the strategy of the initiative.

In the Given Foundation Lecture at Wilson College,
Claire Boothe Luce, an observer often in the past prov-
en notable for her courage and clarity of vision, explored the problem of American morality and nuclear
diplomacy. She assigned much of the moral responsibility for both world wars to our unwillingness to say
in advance that we would intervene. "A good deal of
the blood that was spilled in World Wars I and II must
be laid," said Mrs. Luce, "and is laid by responsible historians, at the door of America's strange morality about
force." And she found us now, with our same strange
morality, committing a similar mistake. In itself, nuclear energy is neither moral nor immoral. As with all
power, it is good or bad *use* that makes nuclear energy
moral or immoral.

Frequently it is women who clearly distinguish the
inner essence of men's actions. It was Senator Margaret
Chase Smith who in September of 1961, as the clouds
over Berlin darkened, noted that Khrushchev, polluting
the air with nuclear blasts, and by the Berlin wall making a frontal attack on humanity and all free men, had
not gained his sudden immunity to action by a new Soviet military advantage, but by the attitude of the new
American president. First she realistically noted that
"the primary determinant for over-all military advantage" is the capacity to wage total nuclear war; then she

quoted Chalmers Roberts whose articles appear in the *Washington Post*, "Power and willingness to use it are fundamental to great nations. That the United States has the power is not doubted in Moscow, by every sign available here. But Khrushchev's latest actions indicate that he doubts the President's willingness to use it."

The "willingness to use it," is the essence of the matter. Free men must stand by their beliefs regardless of the peril. Only thus can they both preserve their own freedom and help the Free World. The fact of our power must be integrated into our diplomacy to back our beliefs, or the sun will set on free civilization. Force is neutral, as Mrs. Luce correctly comments. It is as available to Russia for the enslavement of mankind as to us for the support of free men and our own national existence. Our moral responsibility is to use it for the right.

On this issue, most people, in their private convictions, seem to be ahead of the Administration, and realize that the time has come when we must translate our military superiority into a diplomacy that will confront Communism at each attempted aggression. So long as we hold our decisive superiority, the Communists will back down and the cause of freedom and peace will advance. But if the present policies of drift continue, in a very few years we may lose this advantage—and both our own existence and that of the Free World will be doomed.

7

SUBLIMITED WAR

THERE IS PROOF of the effectiveness of the strategy of initiative; it worked for us in the past, the very recent past under Secretary Dulles; and the Communist powers, in effect, admitted that it worked. Today it is American misjudgment that gives the Soviet Union its successes. It is a failure of Western understanding. It means that we may yet tragically have to "salvage defeat" from what could have been victory.

Because of our determination in the mid and late nineteen-fifties to choose and use our own weapons and our own battlefields (the Eisenhower-Dulles strategy), the Soviet Union was deterred not only from nuclear war but even from Korea-style conventional wars, and Khrushchev made the success of the American policy a part of Communist realism in 1956, 1959, and even in 1961. In those years, before Communist Party Congresses, he explained that open war was no longer "inevitable," as earlier Communist doctrine had held. Henceforth, he said, "wars of liberation," sublimited wars in other words, would be the order of the day. His statement was a realistic and predictable response to America's nuclear advantage and, most importantly, our stated willingness to use it—Dulles' deliberate policy of nuclear strategy.

Meanwhile, however, many in our own country could not believe the success of our nuclear strategy. Army Chief of Staff Maxwell Taylor, during this period, was calling for vastly expanded *conventional war strength* with massive air transport support. His obvious concern was that the new Communist strategy would be one of limited, rather than sublimited war. In such a strategy, he envisioned our conventional forces being directly challenged, perhaps at several points simultaneously. General Taylor's book, *The Uncertain Trumpet*, failed to heed Khrushchev's actual words (referring to "wars of liberation," i.e. *sub*limited war) and made no close examination of Communist guerrilla warfare methods or what would be needed to prepare for the sort of special, sublimited warfare operations we now face in Southeast Asia.*

The fact which later became plain was that Khrushchev's new strategy in no way envisioned matching his divisions against our divisions, even on a limited scale. The full definition of his "wars of liberation" indicated that Khrushchev's real plan was to leapfrog our conventional-force alliance system, subvert countries, embark on guerrilla war—not with divisions but with squads and less—and conduct this type of warfare not directly against us, but against allies and through civil war.

As Chairman of the Joint Chiefs of Staff, Admiral Arthur Radford wanted the Army to assume an increased role in training allies and concentrating on military advisory missions. Some military men, however,

——

*Since this was written, General Taylor has been appointed Chairman of the Joint Chiefs of Staff. Surely the author of a book so very critical of our policies in the 1950's would feel that the same type of hard look at present policies is in order, and would welcome a dialogue on them.

felt this was a degrading activity; although, as actuality has since then thoroughly indicated, guerrilla warfare such as in Vietnam can best be met by its own indirect methods. Admiral Radford also realized that our military and nuclear superiority could deter levels of violence which escalated beyond sublimited war. Unfortunately, however, it was General Taylor's uncertain trumpet on sublimited war rather than Admiral Radford's clear call to action against war by proxy that set the tone for the new President—making impossible a strategy of initiative, paralyzing our new leaders with fear of mass land encounters and escalation and almost completely ignoring the advantages that could be ours because of our general superiority.*

Why did it happen? Why did we not fully foresee and forestall Communism's new form of warfare? Obvious reasons can be found in the role of the military. Military leaders are criticized extensively whenever they enter into political discussions, whenever they speculate on the political effects of a military program; in short, whenever they stray from the field of military maneuvers, weapons, and tactics. Had we understood that the military, composed of highly intelligent citizens with a broad grasp of our military potential and future needs, were well-equipped to make meaningful recommendations for policy, the chances are that accelerated efforts in many areas where we later tried frantically to make up for lost time would have been undertaken when they should have been—years ago.

---

*Taylor, during this time, was predicting that conventional rather than sublimited war was the Communist strategy for the late 1950's and early 1960's. Radford, on the other hand, looked to a new initiative and a new role for the army in training our allies for indirect aggression.

Our military experts cannot work in a vacuum. If we separate them from consideration of the political and psychological implications of military strategy, we cannot feel justified in criticizing them when they fail to anticipate needed programs. In the 1950's the Army introduced a most imaginative ranger training program, but it never applied these doctrines fully in its training of our allies.

A most farsighted proposal, however, did emerge in March, 1961 and was circulated in the Pentagon by the Army's chief of Research and Development, General Trudeau. The author of this memorandum recommended a stepped-up training program in guerrilla warfare for *all United States conventional forces,* an accelerated training program in foreign underdeveloped countries, and the utilization of Communist defectors currently in this country. He said that "the doctrine for countering Communist guerrilla warfare should first be developed on a regional basis . . . [using] SEATO, the Rio Pact, and NATO." Yesterday was the time to prepare ourselves for tomorrow's sublimited wars, in which our own citizens would be active participants.

How should this have been done? By setting up guerrilla training schools in every American combat command, or in strategically located schools serving the same purpose. All combat troops could have been sent to these schools during training periods and made thoroughly familiar with the Communist principles of sublimited warfare. The plan was finally in part implemented at President Kennedy's insistence in early 1962. But no highly developed technique has yet been put into effect in the essential area of troop education for guerrilla warfare, although our experience in such

World War Two theatres as Burma would have formed an excellent core for such a program. In Burma our guerilla battalions were most effective in harassing and delaying Japanese forces. Another opportunity, overlooked or at least not exploited to the full, is the utilization of Communist defectors with actual training in Communist tactics. The free world is not poor in this respect. Cuban refugees, most lately and in abundant numbers, would have constructive aid to offer, if approached. Our allies too, afford an avenue of aid: the French, for example, fought a guerilla war in Indo-China, and in Algeria; the Philippine army was outstandingly successful in the early fifties against the Communist-inspired Huks; the British had experience in Malaya.

Nevertheless, although a training program encompassing Special Warfare, the utilization of Allied experience, and the inclusion of all American conventional forces should have been developed, recommended, and implemented long ago, it is at least satisfying that finally today special warfare is no longer being neglected. Progress in developing sublimited warfare capabilities has been rapid over the past year. But there is still a gap between tactical development and strategic application.

Yet while this Administration, led by President Kennedy, has become deeply interested in guerrilla warfare,* there has been a tendency to isolate it and assign it a purely defensive function. There has been a failure to recognize that it was the successful nuclear strat-

---

*Rep. Dan Flood (D. Penn.), a member of our Defense Appropriations Subcommittee has recognized the importance of stepped up guerilla training for some years now. He has actively espoused implementation of the type of step currently being planned and put into operation.

egy of Eisenhower and Dulles that forced the Communists to narrow their aggression to sublimited war, although Secretary McNamara, in effect, admitted this fact in a statement before the Senate Armed Services Committee in mid-January, 1962: "To the extent we deter the Soviet Union from initiating these larger wars, we may anticipate even greater efforts on their part in the sublimited war area." It is essential to realize, therefore, that a Communist-initiated sublimited war is part of over-all Communist strategy. We cannot proceed as if sublimited warfare were to be the one form of Communist aggression we shall face. That some of our leaders do, however, make precisely this assumption may have been indicated recently by President Kennedy, who reportedly said he would bet nine to one that indirect, sublimited aggression involving guerrillas would be the most likely form of warfare in this decade.* The fact is, however, that the Communists adopted this form of warfare, as we have seen, during our own Phases Two and Three, when we had a preponderance in nuclear advantage and the Dulles strategy of selective retaliation was in the background. But if we approach Phase Four, in which the Communists hope our nuclear lead will diminish and finally disappear— and particularly if we are under the sway of leaders proclaiming the "underdog" policy as if Phase Four were already upon us—the Communists will escalate to vastly enlarged fields of aggression.

Current measures specifically oriented to consideration of guerrilla warfare are in many ways excellent, but only as far as they go. A board of thirteen general offi-

---

*See *Army* magazine, March, 1962, which refers to President Kennedy's reported remark, p. 28.

cers meeting at the Army Warfare Center, and headed
by Lieutenant General Hamilton Howze, recommended
in January, 1962, that the United States:

(1) set up orientation courses for all combat officers of
the rank of colonel and above;
(2) indoctrinate all eight* Army divisions in the United States in guerrilla and counter-guerrilla concepts, techniques, and weapons;
(3) expand counter-guerrilla courses at the four Special Warfare Centers at Fort Bragg, Bad Tölz, Germany, Okinawa, and the jungle school in the Canal
Zone; and
(4) form additional Special Force groups with specific
area assignments.

In addition, in the past year, an office of Special Warfare, directly under the Chief of Staff of the Army, was
established; an accelerated training and education program went into effect; and plans were formulated to
increase the number of special forces personnel. Also,
in crisis areas such as Vietnam, the Military Assistance
Advisory Groups (MAAG), which exist in over forty
countries, were supplemented by a Special War Task
Force specifically competent in guerrilla operations.
These MAAGs, however, are an example of a good idea
weakened by poor planning. In Vietnam, right into
1962, the mission work was geared for another Korean-
type war. That war, after 1951, settled down to something closer to World War I, with long trench lines,
sand-bagged bunkers, and massive artillery and mortar
duels. Thus, according to Bernard B. Fall, in his book
on the Indo-Chinese war of 1946 to 1954, *Street Without Joy*:

---
*Currently ten divisions.

. . . In South Vietnam . . . where United States training methods have had the time to take hold, their effects have produced an army which resembles strikingly that of South Korea. Unfortunately, the terrain conditions under which this new-born army now has to operate are very much different from those of Korea, solidly anchored on two seas and provided with a network of alternate south-north roads and railways. More importantly, the *enemy* itself follows organization patterns which are totally different from those of the Chinese Reds and North Koreans.

But far more important than any of the tactical or technical improvements that have been made, is the key problem of treating each crisis as though it were an isolated case and not intricately tied to the continuous cold war picture. For example, a crisis develops in Vietnam and the Special Forces needed to counter it are pulled out of Okinawa. They are also pulled out of Bad Tölz, Germany. Furthermore, they are pulled out of the Caribbean, and out of Fort Bragg, so that only a skeletal cadre of professionals remains even in that key training command in North Carolina. That Special Forces were needed in Vietnam was obvious. The widespread withdrawal, however, has implications for the rest of the world. All four centers in existence were promptly and effectively tied up by the fighting in Southeast Asia. What realistic policy could we expect to follow in Chile, or any Latin American country—in the Congo, or any country in Africa, and so on all around the world—if another sublimited crisis suddenly develops?

Again, the pressing need is for an inclusive strategy, one upon which we can base all lesser strategies and specific tactics.

Just as the Communists view sublimited war as an intermediate stage leading to a broader application, so too must we consider it. Khrushchev has made it abundantly clear on numerous occasions that "wars of liberation" are waged as "sacred;" that they are religious wars of the secular religion at the core of the Communist drive to ultimate world revolution. On January 6, 1961, he said ". . . a liberation war, a war of independence waged by the people . . . is a sacred war. We recognize such wars; we have helped and shall continue to help peoples fighting for their freedom." Communists have employed variations on this theme from the beginning. Guatemala, Indonesia, and Indo-China immediately come to mind. Mao Tse-tung's prolonged and ultimately victorious struggle in China from 1928 to 1948 is a prime example, just as Mao's doctrine is the guerrilla's bible. The Communists will not change in their attitude toward guerrilla wars. With them, each one is only a piece in the great mosaic, a part of the total design.

The mechanics of sublimited operations are only one small facet of an immense *situational* pressure, constantly and cleverly manipulated by the enemy. At every outbreak we should understand *why* we are involved in that particular war—in whatever capacity we choose to wage it; be it in a military assistance capacity, a limited participation role, or as active participants. Is it merely a delaying action, or a deterrence, or a containment technique? Are we waging it with liberating intent, or only the purpose of destroying the enemy's attack, or because of existing treaties or agreements that we must honor? Whatever the reason of the moment, the ultimate justification should be—in fact, must be—in terms of our own over-all goal, just as the Communists act in terms of theirs. We must see it as one more step in diminishing Communist power wherever it exists, of preventing Communism from consolidating further areas of control, and above all, as part of our struggle for national existence, for survival of our values, for the lives of all free men.

Our actions to date seem to be geared only to isolated bits of geography. We have been concerned with preventing Communist control in some specific location—Southeast Asia, Latin America, or Africa. And even as techniques designed to secure mere geographical units, consistency in action has faltered. Our policies in Vietnam for example, contrasted notably with those in Laos, where our actions were based upon the naive notion that the risks of setting up a government in coalition with Communists were worth taking. Some of our leaders have even believed that Laos was simply not important. One architect of Far Eastern policy allegedly stated, "It doesn't matter much to us, one way or another, what happens in Laos."

Although unappreciated by the State Department, Laos cannot be isolated from overall strategy considerations, and therefore it *does* matter what happens in that country. The key to any strategy of initiative is a response to aggression at the times and places and with the weapons of our own choosing. The foundation of our strategic doctrine must be that we cannot win a war—nuclear, conventional, or sublimited—by defensive tactics, which allow the enemy privileged sanctuaries and special advantages. The tragedy of our present struggle in South Vietnam is that we—with vastly improved tactics—are following a defensive strategy through which we have handed neighboring Laos to the aggressor and restricted our struggle in Vietnam by impossible limitations. If we continue this approach to sublimited aggression, we are doomed to eventual defeat. In regard to our present Southeast Asian policies, our strategy gap is appalling and is endangering the security of the entire area.

Our strategy gap in Southeast Asia, however, results from far more than our lack of a doctrine for taking the initiative in sublimited war. This gap results from a failure to grasp the strategic significance of the key terrain features of the Southeast Asia mainland. In 1954, we faced a crisis in the Red River valley and Dien Bien Phu. Admiral Radford, as Chairman of the Joint Chiefs of Staff, understood that the tremendous power of the Seventh Fleet gave us the capability of sealing off the key mountain passes into the valley. He was anxious for us to intervene at that time and halt the Communist expansion before it fully breached the eastern reaches of the Himalayan mountains—a key defensive terrain feature. The Army Chief of Staff, General Ridgeway, however, was convinced that it was not practical for us to make a stand at that time and argued that we would become involved in a war worse than that in Korea. General Taylor, his successor, followed the same approach.

Both Ridgeway and Taylor are oriented towards Europe where autobahns and highways played an important part in World War II. On the other hand, Brig. Gen. Rothwell H. Brown, now retired, spent a career in the Far East with Stilwell, later with the Marshall mission, and still later, from 1956 to 1959, in Laos. Unhappily, his thinking was seldom in step with that of either the generals experienced in European warfare, or with State Department policies dominated by exaggerated fears of escalation. He was convinced that Laos was and is strategically and militarily defensible in spite of what has been written to the contrary. He saw Laos as the essential strategic buffer separating Red China, North Vietnam and the other countries of Southeast Asia. General Brown's views, if correct, tend to explode many myths about the Southeast Asia mainland, and this is why I think it so tragic that his views about sublimited war have not been heard. Brown made a close study of the earlier French military failures there, and found that they had always tried to defend the more difficult lowlands and delta areas. They failed to block the few mountain passes which could have prevented the flow of supplies and money to Ho Chi Minh for his aggressive actions. Brown points to Dien Bien Phu as the classic tactical failure where the French tried to hold the "bottom of the soup bowl" and gave up the great mountain ring around the area.

When North Vietnam was lost to the Communists following the Geneva accords of 1954, the great strategic barrier north of the Red River valley was lost to the allied cause. Brown was quick to see and to argue that the United States and its allies, after 1954, had to rely on a still difficult secondary barrier to Communist expansion: the mountain barrier which runs just north of the 17th parallel, across the northern boundary of Laos, and from there on to the northern junction of Laos, Burma, and Thailand. These mountains, not the often shallow Mekong River, are the key to the defense of the area. The Communists knew this, but Washington did not see it this way.

As General Brown has written:

A glance at any relief map in any good atlas will show clearly that below the mountains of Laos and west of the mountains along the coast of Viet Nam, there lies a great alluvial plain capable of tremendous agricultural development, but certainly lacking in major military defensive positions. Therefore, it is quite clear that once the mountain barrier is breached, the problem of defending the heartland of Southeast Asia becomes exceedingly difficult.

Plainly, to try to defend the Southeast Asian mainland, by trying to hold defensively this great alluvial plain, would be to repeat the classic mistake of the French—trying to hold the bottom of the soup bowl after giving up the great mountain barriers without a fight. Yet, when we sent our troops to Thailand, it appeared that if we decided to intervene in Laos, we would have to do it through the bottom of the soup bowl.

Once the mountains are penetrated, the prizes of Southeast Asia open to the Communists. General Brown warned, before the coalition government was formed, that the Communists, if in control of Laos, could place their agents along the whole border of the country and commence the softening-up process of all nearby countries. So long as the Communist forces were held north of the mountains, General Brown argued, Laos was acting as a great sponge through which the Communists had to penetrate before their agents could reach Bangkok, Saigon, the Malay Peninsula, and the vast population of overseas Chinese who control such important business interests throughout Southeast Asia. General Brown argued that once Laos fell militarily, or went towards a Communist dominated coalition government, neutralist Cambodia would soon throw its full weight on the Communist side and afford them sea and river routes to the hinterland so that they would not have to use the more difficult mountain routes. He argued that the passage of Laos into Communist hands would cause a rapid deterioration of the position in South Vietnam; that the cost to the United States from a military and economic point of view could become astronomical. Likewise, the position of Thailand would become increasingly tenuous without even the weak barrier of the Mekong River as a defensive position. After some months the Communists would again be in a position to send their many agents and arms through Thailand into the Malay Peninsula, which now has been pacified only after twelve years of war when the Thai government sealed off its southern provinces as a sanctuary for the Malayan Communists. A linking-up of Indonesia and Red China might not be long in coming after these catastrophes, and Burma would be very vulnerable. India would be next. As General Brown has written:

And so we see that from the mountains of Laos, the evil spreads in ever-widening circles. With India either Communist or really neutralized, the great Communist encirclement outlined by Lenin and first placed in execution would have swung from China through Southeast Asia across India and before long it would have penetrated deeper and deeper into Africa.

It is a very strange thing that such a small, poverty-stricken, totally innocent country should have become such a tremendous keystone in the arch of independence and freedom for so many people. But its mountains and its jungles, which create a barrier which must be penetrated before the riches of Southeast Asia can be seized, make this country the most strategically critical country in this whole vast area.

The progression of Communist conquest as outlined above is probably inevitable if Laos falls completely into Communist hands. The speed with which the total conquest would be consumated is, of course, difficult to judge . . . The cost of the retension of Laos is infinitesimal in comparison with the cost of trying to regain Southeast Asia after it is lost.

General Brown's voice has been one crying in the wilderness. His prophecies are all too quickly coming true, but it is still not too late. From his vast knowledge of Southeast Asia, he believes that an end to the hostilities in South Vietnam and any Communist hostilities in Laos could be brought about through military pressures by the United States Seventh Fleet—if it were employed against Haiphong, Hanoi, and the whole Red River valley stronghold. Here is the privileged sanctuary. Here is the source of all Communist power in South Vietnam, Laos, and North Vietnam. Here is a sanctuary vulnerable to aircraft carrier task forces. All along, General Brown has believed that if there was an escalation by the Red Chinese, the bulk of any ground forces which would have to be committed could be drawn from our SEATO allies. Noting that the Chinese have had four or five years of famine and that Soviet Russia has withdrawn industrial support and technical support, Brown feels that if helicopter forces were employed and then backed up immediately so as to seal off the mountain passes leading from China to North Vietnam, the area could undoubtedly be held without too much difficulty against any Chinese Communist onslaught.

We cannot meet the threats of the Communists' so called "wars of liberation" until we close the strategy gap and develop sound doctrine on the strategic level. Fortunately we have, on the tactical level, made splendid strides in the development of sound doctrine, and this leads to a more detailed consideration of South Vietnam.

South Vietnam illustrates how our foreign policy on sublimited war must include three broad areas of action. The political sphere concerns our relations with the internal population of the country in question. It will take more than attempts by our Special Forces to instill in the nations of a particular region the desire to support their government. The enemy is proficient both in propagandizing and terrorizing the peoples of the backward nations. In South Vietnam, for example, it was estimated that forty per cent of the population was either pro-rebel or simply anti-government.

Why?

Some observers blame the South Vietnamese government. They point to the highly personalized and mandarin-like role of Ngo Dinh Diem, alleging that his regime has roused the indignation of the Vietnamese people and will not win their support until it drastically reforms itself on a more democratic basis. There is merit in this contention, but it seems doubtful that it was any major reason for Vietnam's lack of mass popular support for its anti-Communist forces, although in Western terms, the Diem regime certainly was neither democratic nor incorrupt. On the other hand, the Communists were neither saintly, sincere, humane, or notable for other virtues. Virtue in Vietnam was not a part of the contest. That, in fact, was precisely the problem.

Vietnamese peasants, unaware of politics, ignorant of the true nature of Communist slave states, were, like any desperate people, ready to go along with whomever appeared strongest. The Communists, the Viet Cong, struck terror by assassinating government and police officials, plus thousands of citizens. The peasants decided Viet Cong was strongest, and so they went along.

Then in March of 1961 came our own first effective action against the terror. It was a humane measure, with decent protection of life, hope, and labor, and understandable in those terms to even the simplest. It was also intelligent military procedure. Called "Operation Sunrise," this tactic provided for the evacuation of all villagers from territories controlled by the Viet Cong. The villagers' old huts, which might have sheltered Communist guerrillas, were burned and their former owners were given new accommodations in "strategic villages" where they could be protected. In safety, able at last to sow and reap in relative peace, the villagers entered a new existence. At the same time the insurgents were isolated from their sources of pillage and supply, prevented from propagandizing or terrorizing new recruits, and cut off from former channels of intelligence information. Most important of all, the peasants began to have a chance for a new point of view. The key to every situation of sublimited warfare is popular support, which hitherto has been almost invariably won by the Communists through their ruthless combination of propaganda and terror. A people cannot resist lies if there is no way to see the truth; they cannot hold out against terror if they have no protection. In Vietnam a strong and realistic step was taken toward developing measures which may strike at the very heart of Communism's success with sublimited warfare. At the same time special measures were stepped up against the insurgents. They were harassed much as they themselves had harassed government forces and villagers. Being a guerrilla became extremely dangerous, as it had before been dangerous to be a loyal citizen. Use of helicopters as troop-carriers was an example of an effective new device to bring government pressure quickly to bear on the insurgent forces wherever they were found.

Such operations, to be effective, must embrace both propaganda and psychological action directly among the people—propaganda, through such activity as USIA programs;* and psychological action through individual relations between the indigenous forces and the population. For example, government troops must be educated to understand the reasons for respecting private property and the importance to themselves of popular support. Supplying medical aid when needed is one way; repaying a necessary acquisition of native stores with more than the amount taken is another. And whenever such actions are performed, they should be made known through USIA and other media—a policy not now being followed by the USIA—so that the people may know they have nothing to fear from government forces, while, on the other hand any transgression against the population should be punished, and with as much public knowledge as possible.

Roger Hilsman, State Department Director of Intelligence and Research, delivered a notable speech in

---

*Unfortunately, USIA policies today are not geared to this type of approach. If their programs are to become effective in such sublimited warfare areas as Vietnam, they must re-orient their thinking toward a "hard sell" propaganda line, wherein U.S. interests or the interests of the government we back are the prime consideration.

California in August of 1961, recommending a significant tactic which was finally implemented on a limited scale the following March in South Vietnam. Briefly, the tactic calls for dividing the country under attack into sectors, each of which is patrolled by a small, self-sustaining unit of men who are in constant communication with central headquarters. When contact is made with the enemy, heaquarters is notified; so too, are the surrounding units in contiguous sectors. Headquarters dispatches helicopters and paratroops behind the enemy, and all units converge and destroy him. Once this is done, the area is consolidated and the process repeated. In this fashion, sector by sector, the country is purged of guerrilla forces.

In spite of these excellent beginnings, the final countermeasures to defeat the Communist attack on South Vietnam will not be easy nor will they produce quick results. Central to the problem is what Bernard Fall calls "the active sanctuary" which, in this case as well as in the Laotian situation is Communist North Vietnam. "The active sanctuary," Fall points out in his previously mentioned book, ". . . is a territory contiguous to a rebellious area which, though ostensibly not involved in the conflict, provides the rebel side with shelter, training facilities, equipment, and—if it can get away with it—troops."

The prime means of penetrating an active sanctuary is to launch counter-offensives behind enemy lines, recognizing no borders. In the case of Vietnam this means making the price of surviving in North Vietnam as high as the sector plan makes it in South Vietnam. Such penetrating, behind-the-lines offensives can originate either across the border separating North and South

Vietnam by use of the indigenous South Vietnamese forces, or by sending American naval forces to establish a beachhead along the coast of North Vietnam to provide supplies and equipment, expert advice and assistance to landings of South Vietnamese forces, which could then recruit guerillas of their own among the population.

Naval forces can thus become a decisive factor in any guerrilla war waged on territory bounded by water. Establishment of a beachhead by the Navy could serve both to isolate the "active sanctuary" of North Vietnam and to help close off the retreat of the Viet Cong as they are flushed out of South Vietnam. At the same time the Navy's small boats could establish contact with anti-Communist forces along the coast and serve as floating bases of supplies, equipment, and medical aid.

This limited use of the Navy, however, is not meant to indicate that the Navy, Marines, or Air Force should get deeply into guerrilla warfare. This is the domain of the Army. The diversity of planning that usually arises as a result of other services' attempting to "get into the act"* only adds to the confusion of already complex undertakings. Marine helicopters should be turned over to the Army's control, and where small boats or other types of naval equipment are needed in inland waters, these too, wherever possible, should be placed under the command of the Army. Only in undertakings which require establishment of a beachhead, should Naval or Marine forces be used. Guerilla warfare is highly specialized, and should therefore come under the purview of one service exclusively—the Army.

_____

*A notable instance was the Air Force development of its own rifle (the Ar-15) for use in sublimited warfare.

Another means of dealing with sublimited warfare when an active sanctuary is being used is to adopt the Communist device of a "wall," one whose object, however, is to keep aggressors out, not would-be escapees in. Highly charged barbed wire along the dividing frontier is a useful device, reinforced by strategically placed ground units and by helicopter or light-fighter aircraft patrol. This is similar to the Navy's use of CAP in sea operations. In fact, if a beachhead is established with American Naval forces, then the Navy vessels in the area can very easily supply the needed patrol, equipped with appropriate strafing capabilities.

Difficulties of a wall are that the dividing frontier may cover too large an area, or may be composed of dense jungle. In the former case, a complete wall is obviously impractical, but a partial wall can effectively contain those sections through which guerrillas are most apt to penetrate. In the eventuality that the area to be walled is covered with jungle, the recently developed defoliation techniques may ultimately offer a solution. Recent experiences have found them far from satisfactory, but more sophisticated future techniques may see them playing a useful role. Once the border has been sealed and is effectively patroled, and the "active sanctuary" is at the same time being penetrated by beachhead or behind-the-lines incursions, the process of flushing out enemy guerrillas by the sector plan can proceed at top speed.

It is disheartening that the excellent initial progress being made in sublimited warfare in Vietnam has been nullified by our strategy gap. It is particularly hard to understand this difference because even if tactics of sublimited warfare were indeed a matter of dealing with mere geographical units—as it is not—the policy of applying one method to Vietnam and another to Laos would appear beyond the possibilities of reason. Geographically Laos has a long border on the western side of Vietnam, and any attempt to seal Vietnam must include preventing North Vietnamese from using this Laotian territory to penetrate South Vietnam. The absurdity in this case is that the United States, while acting in South Vietnam, at the same time decided to press for a "neutral" Laos, refusing support to pro-Western forces, and allowing continued military conquest by the Communists. Although South Vietnam and Laos are both under attack from the same source, North Vietnam—which is training and equipping, with Soviet and Chinese support, the Pathet Lao in Laos and the Viet Cong in Vietnam—nevertheless in Laos we became committed to the establishment of a popular front government, even withdrawing aid from Boun Oum as pressure on him to accept this objective.*

At the same time, we accelerated our military operations in South Vietnam, apparently determined to prevent a Communist takeover. But in *both* Laos and Vietnam the Communist objective is obviously the same—to gain control of the Southeast Asian peninsula!

The effort to establish a coalition government in Laos and to neutralize that country was never likely to improve the prospects of saving even Laos itself from Communism. The proposed "neutral" government from the beginning was to consist of anti-Communists, "neutralists," and Communists under the direction of a

---

*In June, 1962, the much sought-after coalition government was formed—notably lacking, however, Prince Boun Oum as one of the premiers.

"neutralist" prince whose royal half-brother was the leader of the Communist Pathet Lao and a member of the Communist Party of North Vietnam. The key ministries of Defense and Interior would thus be in "neutralist" hands—neutralist in the Communist sense. This does not mean that the desire to neutralize Laos would have been foolish if it could have been a *genuine* neutralism. Denial of Laotian territory to Viet Cong guerrillas would have facilitated the defense of South Vietnam. *Genuine* neutralization of Laos would have created a buffer between Communist China and North Vietnam and our ally, Thailand. However, it should have been obvious from the first that the genuine neutralization of Laos was impossible. It depended not only on forcing a coalition which would be dominated by internal Communists, but on the faith in whose name we insisted on that coalition—a Soviet pledge to support neutralization.

The astonishing blindness of men of good will to the Soviet record of broken promises never ceases. We are following a strategy of contradictions, one which, unless we rediscover both reason and conscience, may in the end allow the extinction of men of good will throughout the globe, while those who implore us to recover our values and use our strength will go unheeded until it is too late.

8

THE COMMUNIST REGIMES

THERE IS ONLY ONE INSTANCE in history of an entrenched Communist regime having been overthrown by Western initiative. This example is Guatemala, and it is an experience which makes highly doubtful the prevailing fear that "interference" with the Communist rulers of subject peoples could topple the world into war. Guatemala caused a classical display of Soviet temper, replete with charges of American CIA assistance to the anti-Communist Guatemalan insurgents who effected the successful coup. The Soviet display over Guatemala was scarcely less dramatic than Khrushchev's threats to "hurl missiles" on America should there be any interference with the Castro dictatorship, threats that were not heard at all when the actual liberation was attempted. The outcome of that venture, however, is history; our own faint-heartedness forfeited success.

To implement successfully any strategy of initiative, the West must revive the brief light that led to success in Guatemala. And to prevent Communism from consolidating further areas of control, existing Communist regimes must be ousted. But if inhibition is the word for our general approach to the use of national power in meeting Communist aggression as it advances into

116

new territory, paralysis is the term when it comes to
developing the firmness of purpose needed to oust Communism where it has become established. Once a Communist regime has seized power, our own procedure has
been to clothe it in legality, "recognize" it as we say,
and effectively preclude ourselves from acting to free the
people over whom Communist tyranny will soon establish its characteristic coercion, regardless of their view of
its nature in the beginning, when propaganda and promises still had their beguilement.

We permit the Communists unbounded latitude in
invading the free world, but we ourselves will not so
much as touch the Communist world. Was there ever a
more incongruous policy for a great nation which itself
owes everything to the values of freedom? The most
shameful example was Hungary, where men and women
marched in front of our embassy calling, "Why don't
you help us?" The more insidious instance, however, is
Laos, a deadly illustration of our lethal inconsistencies.
For example, in March, 1961, President Kennedy, in a
televised news conference, pointed to a map of Southeast
Asia and declared, "We strongly and unreservedly support the goal of a neutral and independent Laos tied to
no outside power or group of powers, threatening no
one and free from any domination. Our support for the
present duly constituted (Boun Oum) government is
aimed . . . entirely at that result." Later, in the press
conference the President said, ". . . if the Communists
were able to move in and dominate this country (Laos),
it would endanger the security of all, and the peace of
all Southeast Asia." The very next month, April, it was
announced that President Kennedy and Prime Minister
MacMillan had decided on a different view of Laos and

the necessity for a coalition government, following the policy whose consequences we have just reviewed. By June of 1962 when the coalition was finally formed, the tragedy of Southeast Asia had been predictable for months. Our policy there was not a deterrent to war, but an open invitation. Adjacent to the same Laos that we were abandoning to Communism was Vietnam, where we had committed troops, and pro-Western Thailand, which had unmistakably warned us of the consequences of our policy in Laos. Rather than seeking to oust Communists from power, we installed them next door to our allies—allies to whom we were pledged in active support!

My great alarm over these developments finally led me, on July 24, 1962, the day after the signing of the Declaration and Protocol agreement on Laos, to write the following letter to Secretary of State Dean Rusk.

The Honorable Dean Rusk
Secretary of State
Washington 25, D. C.

My dear Mr. Secretary:
It is, of course, no secret that grave doubts and deep concern are being expressed in many quarters over the present Laotian situation. I too, as a member of the Defense Appropriations Subcommittee, am deeply troubled. I have been for many, many months.

On the basis of information recently made public concerning the Declaration and Protocol on Neutrality in Laos, the only possible conclusion one could draw is that Laos is being surrendered to the Communists, as Poland was at Yalta 17 years ago.

The oft-expressed fear, now apparently a fact, that Communist forces are being released in Laos to carry on the fight in South Viet Nam, in which 8,000 American troops are now deeply involved, should be sufficient to shake Administration complacency. Obviously, it is not.

I strongly believe that the net effect of this agreement on Laos will be the intensification of war in Southeast Asia and a weakening of the confidence of free Asians in the value of close cooperation with the United States.

The provisions of Article 14 of the Declaration and Protocol appear to confer a veto power on Communist Poland over the policies of the United States and all other signatory powers in relation to Laos. This, I regard as a nullification of the promises of the agreement.

I gravely disapprove of the procedure, presently being followed, which fails to submit the Declaration and Protocol to the United States Senate for ratification as a treaty.

The Congress and the country deserve a full and frank report from you on future American policy toward Laos. You will recall that President Kennedy, on March 23, 1961, told the American people ". . . if the Communists were to move in and dominate this country, it would endanger the security of all, and the peace of all Southeast Asia . . . that quite obviously affects the security of the United States."

I would be interested in receiving from you a plausible explanation of what makes today any different from March 23, 1961.

Other specific questions to which I would respectfully request detailed replies would include the following:

(1) On what tangible facts do you base the expectation, expressed in the Declaration and Protocol, that this agreement will "assist peaceful democratic development of the Kingdom of Laos" and "the strengthening of peace and security in Southeast Asia"?

(2) What provisions, contained in the Declaration, prevent complete domination of Laos by the Communists?

(3) Does the treaty specifically prohibit Communist troops presently in Laos from moving into South Viet Nam?

(4) How would the United States regard a veto by Poland? Would it be looked upon as a barrier to action by the non-Communist signatories of the Declaration? Would it be a barrier to action in the event of a Communist take-over in Laos? Would it prevent action if the practice of dispatching Communist troops through Laos to Viet Nam were continued?

(5) What action would the government of the United States take in the event of a violation of the treaty and in the face of a Polish veto on action?

It is my profound hope that you will draft an early reply to this letter, a reply that I and the American people can only hope will allay our fears about the present direction of Administration policy in Southeast Asia.

Sincerely yours,
Melvin R. Laird, M. C.

With increasing consistency, our policies move us toward a defensive position stripped of initiative.

What is to prevent us—save our own indecision—from adopting the opposite policy, a policy of initiative, a policy of supporting free governments in Communist-bloc countries? From, at the propitious time, ourselves demanding a neutral government to replace the Communists currently in power?

We, as a free nation, supposedly upholding the values of freedom, have let people after people fall into slavery. That it is high time to reverse the fatal policy is beginning to be recognized, even though action still lags. President Eisenhower in his 1957 Inaugural address said, "We cherish our friendship with all nations that are or would be free. We respect, no less, their independence. And when, in time of want or peril, they ask our help, they may honorably receive it." And President Kennedy in his State of the Union message, January 30,

1961, reaffirmed the attitude, ". . . we must never forget our hopes for the ultimate freedom and welfare of the Eastern European peoples."

Is it not obvious that our course of action, if we are to win the great struggle in which we are engaged, must *implement* these promises? Is it not clear by now, after so many terrible lessons, that our only road to survival depends on adherence to our values, in good faith and at all times? Is it not apparent now to even the most wishfully blind, that our course of action must both prevent the Communists from seizing further territory, and maintain the counter-offensive necessary to oust them from the sanctuaries from which they emerge to attack us? And, finally, is not our moral obligation to the captive nations an honorable imperative, that we will disobey at our own peril?

There are several ways to implement strategy in regard to the captive nations, but probably the most promising at present is to arm and *adequately support* cadres from the enslaved countries themselves. The number of anti-Communist refugees at present in the free world is enormous. Senator Lodge on September 14, 1950, in arguing for increased divisions and manpower for the Army, proposed that "the great mass of anti-Communist freedom-loving young men from behind the iron curtain," be used. He said, "Estimates of the number of these men having an effective potential of military service run as high as two million," in this country alone. He also asserted that "in case of war the United States could recruit as many of these young men as we could clothe and equip." In other words, the great majority of them are eager to fight Communism.

Of course many of these defectors have become United States citizens or citizens of other Western countries;

and though they are still staunchly anti-Communist, it is doubtful that large numbers of them would be willing to volunteer for a separate "army of liberation." It is highly possible, however, that under NATO auspices, reserve forces could be established and maintained for eventual use in aiding the people in the captive nations. Such reserve forces should, wherever possible, utilize foreign nationals who have defected from Communist bloc countries. Whatever type of organization we adopt if we mean to support peoples who *would be free,* we must have the means at our disposal to bring about their freedom. We cannot wait for the Hungarians or Poles to begin a rebellion before we decide to train forces that can aid them. Such rebellion would be crushed in a period of weeks, as Hungary so tragically discovered. The time to prepare a "liberating force" is far in advance of the internal action. With such a force in being, the subjugated peoples behind the iron curtain would be given renewed hope. Psychologically such forces would be a reassurance to those who now believe America has abandoned their nation. Practically, it would serve as a reserve, always ready to be transported to, and to fight for, the homelands of those who comprise the force. And we could then turn Khrushchev's own words against him, speaking of freedom and sacred obligation in their true sense: "A liberation war . . . is a sacred war . . . we have helped *and shall continue to help* peoples fighting for their freedom."

As to underdeveloped countries not yet immediately threatened, the indicated course of action is to help them now to prepare for any future guerrilla war. This could be done by setting up MAAG's* with guerrilla

---

*Military Assistance Advisory Groups.

capabilities whose primary job would be to train and advise the indigenous forces in these lands. In addition, regional schools for foreign officers and men who could return to their own countries and assume the job of training their forces, could be established.

Techniques and weapons related to such objectives are beginning to move in the right direction. New techniques are being formulated; lighter and more flexible weapons are being developed—tiny "dart" guns for guerrilla warfare, armed with rocket-propelled darts that are deadly and accurate; new miniature bombs for high altitude strafing; the defoliation chemicals referred to earlier; dye that is sprayed on fleeing guerrillas or on guerrilla hideouts to facilitate recognition when they return to their pose as native villagers; and very light machine guns—to mention only a few of the devices becoming available. Mechanically, we are coming of age in sublimited warfare.

Thus, tactically and politically some sound ideas are at last being advanced and, in some cases, implemented. But all our efforts are nullified by the irrational paralysis which has prevented us from developing our over-all strategy. Hence we are wasting good will, our new weapons, our waning nuclear superiority, our treasury of ideals, truths, and values. Tactics and techniques, ideals and beliefs can be effective only if organized within the rationally evolved order of firm policy, a policy worthy of freedom and of its strongest home, America.

9

POLITICAL STRATEGY

SOMETIMES A SINGLE, seemingly small event can encompass in itself a world of meaning, and a meaning for the world. Such an event, it seemed to me, marked the consideration of the Peace Corps bill in September, 1961. During that consideration, I offered an amendment that would have changed the name of the organization to the "Freedom Corps." My reason then was the motive which finally grew into this book, and into a position of urging advance of the dialogue that must develop in order to resolve the crisis of our civilization. I said then and still believe, "Freedom is the important issue which faces all people throughout the world . . . mere survival under peace is not the important message we wish to deliver to the world."

The issue and concept of Peace Corps versus Freedom Corps should have been and still could be a crucial part of this century's most fateful discussion. Instead, the amendment was rejected on the basis of such off-the-subject reasoning as that of one gentleman who explained that the organization was already widely known as the Peace Corps and that the publicity received under that name could not be repurchased for millions of dollars. The name Peace Corps, he soberly noted, could be equated with "Ivory Soap" and its merchandising impact. Just as Procter and Gamble would not give up the name Ivory Soap because the soap was not, in fact, made of ivory, neither should Congress change the name of the Peace Corps just because of some notion or another about *its* nature. This sort of argument demonstrates a number of unpleasant facts:

So long as good men keep distracting themselves with the political gadgets and details of cold war machinery and tactics, they will be unable meaningfully to debate and resolve cold war objectives and strategy.

So long as we are inhibited from publicly framing our discussion of objectives in terms of genuine meaning, making the distinctions between various priorities, examining their morality, and evolving a coherent structure, we will be doomed to speak to the world in words that may be effective in selling soap, but are clearly insufficient for instilling hope and winning wars.

So long as we stumble and fumble with our words we will stumble and fumble with our wills.

So long as we are unwilling to use every means necessary to further our aims (not prettify or obscure them) in political warfare, we will lose skirmish, battle, war, and world.

It makes little difference if we are superior in spiritual, economic, cultural, and military strengths if we do not believe, speak, and act as though we are. Our great weakness is that we do not believe our own strengths and, at the same time, we misunderstand the true nature of the conflict in which that strength is pitted. Seeking the "let's-talk-it-over" accommodations in which everything is a shade of gray, never black and white, we have eroded our commitments to the self-evident truths of our own history. We find it, therefore, difficult to believe that other peoples may have ideas as strong and unshakeable as ours once were. It has been said that words are the bullets of the Twentieth century. Beliefs are the century's nuclear bombs.

In our time Communism represents an enormous act of faith. Its fallacies and errors lie strewn before the faithful like the never-buried bones of some sacrificial pit—yet the faithful remain faithful. Communism, powered by its faithful, moves relentlessly across the world. Christianity, base of the Western civilization which Communism is seeking to replace, meantime finds its own faithful pulling down their blinds, trying to lock doors, and arguing wishfully among themselves about ways in which the two irreconcilable faiths, Communism and Christianity, can live at peace; never mind which is good and which is evil.

In spite of its accumulated centuries of demonstrated progress toward freedom and solid accomplishment, the West doubts and frets; while the Communists, on the other hand, although they have no shred of evidence that the Communist state will, as its own founding fathers promised, ever wither away, continue unflinchingly to believe that it will. Such an enormous act of irrational faith can, and does, move mountains and manipulate men and events—and will go on doing so until confronted with the effective counter-force of belief whose superior strength is the awareness of its own truth.

Counter-force is never simply counter-action. Effective political warfare demands more than just the political tactics of the USIA in disseminating information. It needs more than the mere exposure of Communist fallacies. It needs more than just a torrential tactical war of words. What it requires is the expression of the West's self-evident truths. It needs a towering statement of belief.

For the United States, effective political warfare must rise from the traditional, deeply-rooted values of Western civilization, not from the window-box plantings of positivism, materialism, or worship of government as anesthetic answer to the basic spiritual ills of human nature. Carlos P. Romulo, retiring from his post as Ambassador to America from the Republic of the Philippines, in February, 1962, told a group of Americans, "If you can really make the American way of life the spiritual way and convince the world that you practice it, it is the way of life that is destined to become not only invincible but always supreme." Here indeed is the base of effective force! Without it, our actions are meaningless. Only from the sincerity of our deepest beliefs can we effectively move to the exposure and defeat of Communism.

The waging of successful political warfare is a task that begins at home. Gerhart Niemeyer has stressed that "citizens who are ignorant of Communism, its nature, ideas, organization, and strategy, are a national liability." Certainly such citizens can cause remarkable confusion about the true nature of Communism! A notable instance was *The Liberal Papers,** the recently published collection of academic studies commissioned by a group of House Democrats headed by Representative James Roosevelt. The day before the book was formally issued, I took the floor along with many of my col-

*Doubleday, 1962.

leagues, to argue against its proposals. Outstanding in its theses were unilateral disarmament, encouragement of socialism as a "competitive" answer to Communism's socialism, and resolution of East-West tensions by compromise—or, in short, tackling the so-called "Communist problem" as really not so much a problem as just a legitimate misunderstanding between sides of equal merit and good will. I specifically took exception to a paper prepared by Professor Quincy Wright, which proposed "strengthening" the United Nations by such means as "recognition by the United States and admission to the United Nations of Red China, both Germanys, both Koreas, and both Vietnams." As I said at the time, "I cannot believe that more than a handful of my colleagues feel that the cold war is a (mere) misunderstanding."

The handful that does feel it is a misunderstanding, however, is an articulate one, made more so by the inhibitions which move many to refrain from debate against it because of the way in which all anti-Communist arguments are now skillfully being made to appear as manifestation of a lunatic-fringe. The memorandum which Senator Fulbright sent to Defense Secretary McNamara in June, 1961, is a good example of the resulting mislabelling, as astonishing as it is inaccurate. In one section of the memorandum, the Foreign Policy Research Institute at the University of Pennsylvania, directed by one of the world's most respected geo-politicians, Dr. Robert Strausz-Hupé,* was associated with fringe groups whose loudest concerns included everything from the fluoridation of water to the explanation

---

*Quoted above, Part I.

of every Communist success as a result of domestic treason. The existence of these groups has been seized upon as a means of discrediting all anti-Communism, all speakers for free enterprise, all proponents of freedom anywhere in the world.

In spite of such attacks, there is an encouraging increase of activities directly involved with making clear the aims, nature, and organization of Communism. Across the country there are seminars, study groups, and civilian-military meetings whose entire purpose is to familiarize Americans with the true nature of Communism. To be sure, there have been abuses of such efforts, although not nearly so many as the abuses of left wing causes infiltrated by Communism. The total of such abuses by the anti-Communist groups is marginal as compared to the value of the programs.

The most frequent criticism I have heard of such groups is that some have countenanced statements in which Communism is equated with socialism, and socialism is in turn equated with the policies and programs of the Kennedy Administration. Such an assertion is, indeed, highly inaccurate. What it reveals, however, is not a need to halt the study of Communism, but the necessity of making the actual nature of Communism better known. Socialism is a way of organizing society and distributing its wealth according to central plans rather than according to individual initiatives. Although socialism requires, to be effective, full force of government controls, including police powers, it is doctrinally committed to applying this force only *after* obtaining the consent of the people subsequently to be subjected to its plans. On the other hand, Communism, although employing socialist forms, begins with the

imposition of dictatorship by the Communist Party itself and—a basic difference—employs force, violence, and
terror as routine and continuous tools of its power.

If the American public were to be successfully prevented from understanding the differences between socialism and Communism, we would vastly complicate
our task of mounting an effective strategy to win the
cold war. We would, among other things, divert our
energies from an un-debatable, weapon-backed tyranny
and dissipate them on a very debatable and electorally
determinable matter of partisan politics. It is for this
reason that such men as General Walker, although im-
passioned in their efforts to combat Communism, have
tragically obscured the task at hand.

But the complications introduced by all such persons
and their groups, such as the John Birch Society, are not
one ounce heavier in responsibility for dividing our
nation at a time when unity is needed, than are the
forces who oppose them with just as untutored and
indiscriminate charges. It is distressing to note that no
more forceful example can be found than the actions of
Senator Fulbright, a former university president and
Rhodes scholar, and chairman of the powerful Senate
Foreign Relations Committee. Surely, with such a background, Americans might have expected more, not less
sophistication, than from General Walker or Robert
Welch? And yet, in Senator Fulbright's widely circulated memorandum to Defense Secretary McNamara,
opposing public discussions of Communism by military
reservists or other service-connected personnel, the Senator's frame of mind was such as to enable him to say:
"Fundamentally it is believed that the American people
have little, if any, need to be alerted to the menace of
the cold war."

What does the Senator mean? Are millions of Americans, who are asking nothing more than to be admitted to the dialogue regarding Communism, to keep silence? Clearly the Senator does not care for the idea of drawing them into discussion. How is his attitude proper in a nation dedicated to freedom of speech?

Eternal vigilance—shrugged off as a cliché by those who agree with Senator Fulbright—is still the price of liberty. We must not condemn ourselves to repeat the mistakes of two past world wars by a policy of "not being alerted" to the dangers of war and aggression today. We must not condemn ourselves to repeat the mistakes of Yalta by continuing to misunderstand our present enemy.

Senator Fulbright's memorandum seeks and finds further reasons for stopping the development of public dialogue on a strategy for the cold war. It is only natural that men whose profession is war would be involved in such discussion, but the Senator's memorandum says, "Perhaps it is far-fetched to call forth the revolt of the French generals as an example of the ultimate danger. Nevertheless, military officers, French or American, have some common characteristics arising from their profession and there are numerous military 'fingers on the trigger' throughout the world."

Not since Revolutionary War times has there been an occasion of a military uprising in America. The military in this country is an element of stability. An informed military is essential in any strategy of political warfare or military deterrence. Certainly the program of informing troops, and especially officers, was a subject which needed study, as was undertaken very ably by a committee under the chairmanship of Karl Bendetsen, and Secretary McNamara should be praised for appointing that balanced and able group. One of its important conclusions, as well as a conclusion of the hearings of the Stennis Subcommittee, was pointed out by S. L. A. Marshall—that troop indoctrination, in order to be meaningful, must be built around training for combat effectiveness. War, in short, is the reason for allowing meaningful discussion to the military.

Officers and men of the Army, Navy, Marine Corps, and Air Force, not only must have an understanding of Communism if they are to function effectively, but they also require a thorough comprehension of all vital international situations. What is called politico-military affairs is recognized as an area of increasing importance. Already noted is the fact that the Army in the 1950's failed to anticipate fully the role of paramilitary operations because of failure to anticipate the politico-military conditions which would develop during the next decade. When some Army officers progressed in this direction, they were told not to enter areas which were the exclusive concern of the State Department! Indeed, had we followed the ideas of General Rothwell Brown, the military man on the spot in Laos, instead of the ideas of the State Department, we would not have been trapped in the present crisis in Southeast Asia. It is true indeed that our military must not dominate foreign policy, but the present trend of downgrading the need to inform the military, and muzzling their own contributions to discussion, is equally dangerous.

The *responsibility* of exploring the issues of the cold war rests upon every one of our citizens. It rests upon doctors, lawyers, housewives, insurance salesmen, industrial and labor leaders, factory workers, farmers, the whole United States population. Maximum freedom of discussion must be allowed. No one should muzzle an opponent or try to overwhelm him into agreement. For example, while this book examines the values on which I believe the future of our society depends, that does not mean that the most courteous of hearings should be denied to persons with socialistic, materialistic, or positivistic leanings. The views of all must be heard and answered. It is only from a genuine public dialogue freely conducted that there can emerge a consensus to give force to our public strategy in this critical time.

Such public dialogue, however, *must* include the understanding of Communism that can come only through comprehensive study. Lack of knowledge about Communist ideology and strategy must inevitably result in consistent failures on the practical level to cope with the Communist threat. Specifically, the nature of Communism must be studied in our schools, under teachers who themselves are experts in the major aspects of the Communist phenomenon. Foundations concerned with using their resources to combat Communism would be well advised to provide funds to establish schools for such teachers throughout the country. School instruction, seminars, town meetings, adult education groups, Chamber of Commerce meetings, labor meetings, all should address themselves to problems of public strategy. A typical agenda should aim above all at clarity and realism:

(1) Know what Communism is;
(2) Recognize Communist strategy;
(3) Comprehend the true nature of the conflict;
(4) Explore what it will take to win the cold war;

(5) Explore our responsibilities to the subjugated peoples in Russia, Red China, and the satellites;
(6) Know our own strength;
(7) Be willing to use our great power to prevent the Communist use of power to overthrow our ideals, institutions, and representative government;
(8) Explore our own values—values beyond those of mere survival.

A public strategy arising from public understanding and unity would, I believe, bring us to the sober conclusion that we must declare and wage political war. Only by political warfare based upon our pre-eminent power position can we destroy the Communist strategy of terror. Khrushchev demonstrated his mastery of the psychological techniques of political warfare by the events he engineered prior to, and at the conclusion of, the recent Twenty-second Communist Party Congress: the commencement of atmospheric tests just before the Belgrade conference of neutralist nations; the conducting of practically the whole nuclear series with no formal announcements of when the blasts would be detonated, of how many there would be, or the megaton strength per bomb; the announcement that a fifty-megaton bomb would be set off on Halloween eve. In addition there was his personal use of propaganda during the Congress. He went to every length to alarm the world over the fall-out question: Would drinking water be affected? Would milk be safe for children? Would the very air be contaminated?

In political warfare, we of the West face a basic problem: we wish to be constructive; the Communists wish to be destructive. The only way we can ever hope to be a positive force for the restoration of peace is to be willing to utilize our strength and power in our dealings, not only with the Communist-bloc nations, but with all the non-Communist nations. Admiral Arleigh Burke has said that "only a great power has those attributes of economic, political, spiritual, military, and psychological superiority that permit it to *determine the course of events* apart from either pure force or pure persuasion." (Italics supplied). The United States is a great power. Today it is undisputedly the greatest. With the proper use of its power throughout the entire spectrum of human actions, the United States *can* control events, but only if it has the will to do so.

The will to win means that first of all there must be an end to irrational policies. It never makes sense to aid an enemy, yet we do exactly that. Yugoslavia is a Communist nation, even though it has ostensibly broken ties with Moscow. There is no doubt that in any war between Communism and the Free World, Yugoslavia would be on the side of the Communists. Nevertheless we extend aid in the form of jet trainers to Yugoslavia. Why? Primarily because we are under the impression that this is a territorial war we are fighting—that we are dealing in mere units of geography. We feel that economic or military aid to Tito might possibly result in strengthening his stand against Moscow, but we do not take heed of the fact that this aid will strengthen his position as World Communism's spearhead, holding Yugoslavia and pointing against the West. We use somewhat similar reasoning in our dealings with other Communist-bloc nations. In other words we are trying to buy something that is not for sale—Communist disunity in its aim of world conquest. In our dealings with Communist–bloc nations, we have to face the reality that our traditional Western ground rules do not apply, and that the amateurish psychological technique of winning them over by friendship or humanitarian methods is not only useless, but is to them a subject of ridicule, merely proof of capitalist weakness and decadence.

A determined effort to influence the people behind the iron curtain is long overdue. The Communist doctrine that the Free World is for them a "war zone," while the countries behind the iron curtain are for us a "peace zone" must be reversed. As reviewed in the previous chapter, proper techniques, coupled with adequate support could one day result in some of those nations freeing themselves from their hated masters. We cannot set out to foment revolutions, but we can stand poised and prepared to take advantage of any internal weakness in the Communist empire. Once millions of Americans marched to the Battle Hymn of the Republic, "As He died to make men holy, let us die to make men free." This spirit, recaptured in our time when the whole world is half slave and half free, could shape the future of free humanity.

Policies we adopt with respect to Communist nations will have repercussions in the non-Communist world as well. Because political warfare is not selective we have to face the problem of our relations with, and policies toward, non-Communist nations, whether neutrals or allies.

Our approach to neutrals now is rather distorted. We tend to view them as the most articulate spokesmen of world opinion, and we are sensitive about the image we display to them and through them to the world, as if a favorable world opinion were the ultimate good. The fact is, however, that the neutrals themselves are also in the struggle for survival, and if they are to cater only to animal survival, we merely do them harm if we aid and abet them.

We must openly offer *our* approach to life, our values, our beliefs. In political warfare against the Communists within the uncommitted nations, we must not fight the Communist fallacy with other social or economic fallacies. Theodore Roosevelt pointed out basic ingredients of our system when he said, "Americanism means the virtues of courage, honor, justice, truth, sincerity, and hardihood—the virtues that made America. The things that will destroy America are prosperity-at-any-price, peace-at-any-price, safety-first instead of duty-first, the love of soft living, and the get-rich-quick theory of life."

If courage, honor, justice, truth, sincerity, and hardihood—by which Roosevelt meant toughness in pursuit of an ideal—were the ingredients that turned the American dream into reality, is it not just and proper that we should suggest to the underdeveloped nations our principles of success? This would prevent our misleading them into the notions of "inflationary" prosperity-at-any-price or peace-at-any-price, security first instead of commitment to ordered freedom and responsibility, love of soft solutions for economic development, or the get-rich-quick mentality of playing a middle game in search for both our money and Communist money.

Foreign aid in the sense of foreign economic development has become, whether we admit it or not, the top priority of the last three administrations in conducting political warfare. This *priority* is wrong. Although much foreign aid has been highly effective—for example, General Van Fleet's action in Greece and the Marshall Plan to help restore war-torn but highly industrialized

Europe—those plans were part of *long-range over-all* strategy and hence achieved their aim. The recent programs have been of quite opposite quality. Each case has almost invariably been regarded as a unit self-contained and purely in the present, and aid has contributed little in the ultimate design of winning the cold war. Foreign aid should not be used to *buy* nations. It should be used to *reward* nations for long-term allegiance to our side. Foreign aid should not be given as a panacea for a nation's ills; only as highly selective aid is it essential to our strategy and the stability of friendly free governments. Foreign aid should not be presented as a substitute for foreign investment, and it should be withheld in countries opposed to foreign investments or to domestic investments by the private sector. Above all, foreign aid should not be allowed to become a creator of the type of statism that crushes free choice and builds government tyranny.

In the area of economic development, we are waging political warfare against the Communists, with the undeveloped nations as spectators. Eventually we will lose the confidence of these nations if we merely answer the Communist solutions with economic solutions that never worked in our own country, and may very well doom prosperity and certainly limit freedom in theirs.

Colin Clark, the famed Australian economist now in England, has ably noted, for example, present misconceptions concerning economic growth. He points out that "growth at any cost" as a primary objective of economic policy is dangerous; that models of growth, formulated during the post-war period of capital shortage, are out of date now; that the principal factors in economic growth are human, not physical factors; that human factors such as better organization, knowledge, skills, and education, develop slowly; that the classical economists were wise when they saw that the agents of growth were not capital alone but also included land, labor, and enterprise; that loans to underdeveloped countries should not be employed to strengthen author- itarian government and weaken private initiative.* Our aid program to India, which in population equals about half of the uncommitted world, is geared to the very opposite of this caveat.

Peter Bauer, Professor of Economics in the Univer- sity of London, has pointed out how India, especially since 1956, has sharply discouraged savings and invest- ment by its people "by hostile official statements, high taxation, specific controls and prohibitions, expropria- tion of land, sudden acts of nationalization, and mone- tary instability."† Professor Bauer maintains that in our foreign aid policies towards India, we have been in effect pushing that nation towards a completely social- ized economy which will narrow the range of individual choice, instead of giving aid that will advance freedom. Aid to India should be made to depend upon the Indian government's instituting policies to raise living stand- ards—with the sincere aim of developing non-totalitar- ian social forms and evolving a society based on justice and respect of person.

Baffling to many of our allies and sympathizers is our policy of giving aid to friends and non-friends alike. Speaking of Laos, President Ayub Khan of Pakistan, on

---

*In *Growthmanship*, published for the The Institute of Economic Affairs, London, 1961.

†*Indian Economic Policy and Development* (Ruskin House, George Allen & Unwin, Ltd., London, 1961).

a visit to this country, expressed his shock at realizing that we treated friends and non-friends with equal liberality, and added: "The American policy of encouraging neutrality in areas where we know it will operate in the long run against their interests and their friends' interests is considered incomprehensible."*

Until neutrals can decide which of the two great powers will win the cold war, they will postpone choosing sides—condemning our actions on occasion with vehement protest, and only mouthing mild expressions of disapproval at some of the more barbarous Communist "manifestations of good will." In essence, the neutrals have been psychologically "persuaded" by terror: they fear the Communists; they do not fear us nor, apparently, even respect us. Such nations should not in fact "fear" us, in the sense that we might unleash a nuclear holocaust if antagonized by them, or invade their borders, or overthrow their governments. But they should have a healthy respect for the most powerful nation in the world. Respect, however, is never developed for anyone with an underdog complex. Human nature tends to back a winner. If our attitude is not that of a winner, we will find ourselves totally lacking in backers, while the Communists, boasting about their strength and proclaiming the inevitability of their victory, will have the globe trembling at their feet.

The world has been given the impression that we desert our friends and retreat in the face of showdowns— Hungary, Cuba, Laos, and the rest. The quality of our actions on those tragic occasions has already been examined; however, the results went far beyond the actions

---

*To *New York Times* reporter, Paul Grimes, in discussing SEATO's failure to intervene in Laos.

themselves with an impact on a watching world, which judged us and adjusted its loyalties accordingly. In such cases, "image"—that much misused word—does have importance, because at such times our "image" causes the world to alter its own resolves and allegiances. When confronted with an image of a United States uncertain and lacking self-confidence, it is small wonder that we have the strange phenomenon of the "neutral."

How does one then deal with such nations? We cannot treat them as our enemies, for they are not enemies. Indeed they may be important potential friends.

Power can be used directly or indirectly. In dealing with Russia and Red China, the tactic recommended in this book has been one of confrontation, *direct* application of power. While we have our superiority, Communists will back down if confronted in a way that will not allow them to miscalculate. In our dealings with the neutrals, however, we should follow what could be called a "tactic of non-conflict." This is an *indirect* application of power, and should become an integral part of our political strategy.

Such a tactic, for example, could have been applied to India in regard to Goa, where towards the end of 1961, Nehru made clear his intention to use force to "liberate" Goa from Portugal. A request to Nehru to refrain from using force against Goa having met refusal, the next step in the tactic would be to inform the Indian Government that we would not tolerate its military conquest of Goa, and upon the embarkation of military penetration into Goa would cut off our foreign aid to India. At the same time, on the psychological level, it would be made clear to Nehru that the moment he went ahead with his plans, all our forces of information would be used to tell the world of the true nature of India's imperialistic action in Goa. The point here is that the United States as a powerful nation has many means at its disposal short of military action, with which to achieve a desired end and prevent aggression. The tactic of "non-conflict" applied to the non-Communist world would be strong insurance against Communist effort to break down order, cause chaos, and set the scene upon which the Communist dictator most readily arrives.*

In essence this means that the United States would use her power to insure that no "brush wars" break out among non-Communist nations. The Communists, thriving on disorder and chaos, have made inroads in such areas as the Middle East, Africa, Southeast Asia, and our near neighbor Cuba, as the direct result of tensions arising or deliberately created in these areas. In this regard, as in so many others, we have allowed ourselves to be psychologically out-maneuvered. We have become preoccupied with "anti-colonial" and "anti-dictatorship" concepts to the extent that we will utilize power to oust a non-Communist dictator in Cuba and the Dominican Republic, or condemn free-world countries who retain some traces of colonialism, and then allow these same areas to fall under the dictatorial colonialism of the Communist Empire, which is the major colonialism of our time, an imperialism implemented by local dictators who make the Victorian age seem tentative and delicate in contrast.

The "tactic of non-conflict" argues for a reversal of

---

*Strangely enough, we have shown ourselves capable of applying such pressures, as in the recent case of Peru. But, ridiculously enough, we applied them against some of the strongest anti-Communists in the Western Hemisphere.

our basic policy of the "non-use of power." We are now supplying some kind of aid to almost all non-Communist nations, and deplorably, to some Communist nations as well. It is time we made this aid dependent upon commitment to the anti-Communist cause. Otherwise, we are simply bankrupting ourselves while strengthening the enemy. On the other hand, when faced with the choice of committing themselves or of being deprived of some much-needed financial aid, the notion of "neutral status" would lose much of its present appeal.

Some would argue that this policy of "non-conflict" by-passes the United Nations, and hence would destroy any chances of its effectiveness. I would respond that our willingness to act to prevent aggression, and to act unilaterally, is the only hope the United Nations has ever had of developing any effectiveness whatever. The first principle of leadership is to lead. President Truman did not wait for the United Nations to act before ordering our troops committed in Korea to protect that country's freedom. The United Nations then followed.

The overall problem of peace is always the same. Peace, in a time of conflict, follows victory. Victories must be won. To win, to bring and keep the peace, is the challenge we face. Our overriding national goal must be victory over Communism through the establishment of a world in which men can live in freedom, security, and national independence. There can be no real peace short of it! We will have achieved victory when the Communists have stopped trying to dominate the world.

10

COLD WAR ECONOMICS

A WORLD OF PEACE AND JUSTICE cannot indeed be bought. But it does have to be paid for. The highest price is in dedication, and dedication is a quality that cannot be measured in dollars and cents. The *tools* of that dedication, however, can be. In fact, they must be.

Today the tools of our dedication to the struggle against Communism are not measured in a meaningful way. Our defense spending is lumped with all other spending as merely one more massive item in government's use of our tax money, and in that spending virtually all items are considered "urgent." They are sprayed into our legislation like successive blasts from a shotgun. The lack of precision aiming, of rifle-shot determinations targeted to an over-all strategy, is another reflection of the lack of over-all policy. If strategy is ever to be precise, so must be our budgeting—and in the light of predetermined over-all, long-range goals.

We need, as never before, an understandable method of allotting priorities. We cannot afford to spend less than is needed. But we imperil our every purpose if we spend profligately, if we waste our substance. All of our vast wealth is desperately needed by the Free World, to preserve that world. Lesser needs are luxuries. We must separate and order our priorities.

I would specifically recommend the formation of a committee for priorities review. Such a proposal has actually been available for discussion in the dialogue of cold war determinations since 1960, when Dr. William Y. Elliott of Harvard, in a paper prepared for *American Strategy and Strength,** first made it, and it deserves serious consideration, for until it is adopted in meaningful form, we run the risk of squandering the strength on which freedom depends.

Such a committee is envisioned as an independent advisory group to the President. It would be composed of a nucleus of skilled and acknowledged experts in foreign policy, research and development, economics, defense, psychological warfare, sublimited warfare, foreign aid, military assistance, and disarmament. The committee would be an arm of the President, not his antagonist. One of the major difficulties today arises from the Congress' inability to secure information as to the Administration's evaluation of what is needed most and what least, and to determine a realistic order of importance.

Defense spending since 1954 has been relatively stable. Non-defense spending, on the other hand, has almost doubled. Representative George Mahon (D. Texas), Chairman of the House Appropriations Subcommittee on Defense,† indicated this on April 17,

---

AMERICAN STRATEGY AND STRENGTH was a report that grew out of fifty study papers prepared by experts in all fields of foreign policy. The special task force that drew up the report was chaired by Rep. Gerald Ford (R. Mich.). The task force was appointed by the chairman of the Republican Policy Committee, Rep. John W. Byrnes (R. Wisc.).

†The Subcommittee to which I belong and whose findings provided much of the motivation for this book.

1962, in a floor debate relating to the Defense Appropriations bill. He said that defense spending, from 1954 to
1961 increased by only one per cent, while, "non-defense
spending during this 1954-61 period increased by sixty-
five per cent." "If you project this through fiscal year
1963," he went on, "you will find again, according to
the budget estimates, that through that period the increase in defense spending will be twelve per cent above
1954, and non-defense spending will be ninety-four per
cent above non-defense spending in 1954." Plainly, the
great leap in government expenditures has come from
the non-defense sector. Yet the majority of the nation
has been misled into believing that the reverse is true.

Some would argue that the increase of $7.5 billion
since 1961 clearly indicates that the United States was
not adequately prepared two years ago to meet the rising
Communist threat, that our defense expenditures should
have been increased long ago, and that the previous Administration and Congresses did not meet their obliga-
tions adequately in this area. Mr. Mahon anticipated
this reaction: "There has been a very marked change in
the situation which confronted us in the 1950's and the
situation which is confronting us in the 1960's. It is no
criticism of any past policy of the Congress to say that we
have abandoned the level of defense that we had two
years ago and have raised the level of the program to a
higher plateau. A program to acquire a more immediately alert posture to resist aggression was inevitable. It
has no political complexion. It would have come about
sooner or later under any Administration. It happens to
be coming at this time and it is timely."

The defense budget, though in no way commensurate
with non-defense spending, still requires sober consid-

eration for its proper financing. All are agreed that a nation's defense capability rests largely upon the strength of that nation's economy. In two world wars for example, our productive capacity was a decisive factor. In fact, productive capacity is the base for the nation's security effort. Thus, the state of the nation's capacity for defense and the condition of its economy are bound closely together. It is axiomatic that an inflation-ridden, unhealthy economy will not support a strong defense effort. This was recognized in the long-pull concept of the Eisenhower Administration, and endorsed by Admiral Radford before Congress: "Without any reservation, I subscribe to the theory that as military men, in trying to work out plans for the long pull . . . we must take economic factors into consideration. . . ." Added to this may be the point often made by the present Assistant Secretary of Defense, Charles J. Hitch, that all military problems are in a sense economic, in that they involve the most efficient and effective allocation and use of resources.

Thus the state of the nation's economy, especially in the context of the cold war, is of paramount importance. How we allocate our economic resources may determine the outcome of the struggle for the Free World's survival. And certainly the resources we have available will depend upon a strong and dynamic domestic economy. Without this, advances in modernizing our weaponry would be curtailed; maintenance of an adequate standing military force would be threatened; and our commitments around the world would be in jeopardy.

Some students of the economics of national defense point out that a nation's base of industrial mobilization has little effect upon its capacity for immediate retaliation in case of nuclear attack. This of course is true. In fact, this same argument with respect to standing forces has always been true. But, in the situation we face today, the industrial capacity and health of the economy are what make it possible to develop and maintain the standing forces necessary to meet a nuclear attack. Furthermore, if the immediate attack is not successful in ending the war, the question of recovery and the ability to continue to fight, and to win, will depend during each day, week, and month of survival more and more heavily upon the strength of the economic and industrial capacity.

There are few who can disagree with this logic. The disagreement arises in the formulation of policies to implement it. For example, in discussing the resources to be devoted to national defense, the question is more one of priorities, particularly in government spending, than of total cost. Expenditures for national security are a major part of the Federal budget; in fact the defense budget alone accounts for more than half of the total. Yet, as has been shown, the military budget has been relatively stable, forty to fifty billion dollars over the last decade, and at present it is only about ten per cent of our total production of goods and services, the so-called gross national product, the GNP.

In the past we have spent far more. In World War II, for instance, we devoted forty-two per cent of GNP to the defense effort. If necessary, we could do so again. But the real problem is to understand what constitutes defense and national security expenditures—and then in the light of this understanding, to make sensible determination of priorities in our programs of government expenditure. Priority is the central problem. In view of the national concern over world conditions, and the disposition to give more favorable consideration to expenditures for defense purposes, many programs—Aid to Education, Urban Renewal, Mass Transportation, Public Power, Conservation and Flood Control, and River and Harbor development, to mention only a few— are given a national defense orientation by their proponents.

In the Federal Aid to Public Education controversy, for example, its advocates stated that there was a very definite national interest associated with massive aid— as if this could remedy the decline in quality of education resulting from the progressive educationists' approach. Again, in his transportation message of April 5, 1962, President Kennedy said, "An efficient and dynamic transportation system is vital to our domestic economic growth . . . (and) influences both the cost and the flexibility of our defense preparedness."

A strong case can be made for the obvious connection between such proposals of a non-defense nature and their close relation to defense needs and planning. The difficulty, however, is that somewhere a line must be drawn. When these programs are considered along with the mounting direct defense costs, the total of government expenditures—or, to put it another way, the command on the part of government over resource allocation—reaches proportions which must inevitably have far-reaching consequences upon the continued efficient functioning of our private enterprise economy.

At the present time, for example, there is serious concern in many quarters, both private and government, over taxes. Can industry and business earn sufficient income *after taxes* to provide for replacement of plant and equipment as well as for further expansion, whether through retained earnings or through the ability to attract new capital for investment? Industry faces serious problems in this matter. Greater costs without a commensurate increase in profits is crippling industry's ability to compete successfully in world markets. Steel, for example, faces the problem of obsolescence in much of its machinery installed since World War II. Technological advances have made much of this equipment uneconomic when compared with some of the more modern—and thus, more efficient—machinery used by many of American steel's foreign competitors, and by domestic competitors developing newer metals.

The Undersecretary of the Treasury, Mr. Henry Fowler, in an address before the Virginia Industrial Management Conference, in early April, 1962, indicated that the Treasury Department and the Administration were concerned by the fact that corporate profits after taxes had shown no significant increase in the past decade, though corporate sales had increased more than seventy per cent and the gross national product had risen nearly sixty per cent. This statement, interestingly enough, was made before the "crisis" of big steel's price rise. I most heartily agree with the Undersecretary that this situation, if prolonged, bodes ill for the continued efficient functioning and growth of the private enterprise system. It is becoming constantly more evident to discerning Americans, of whatever political and economic persuasion, that all is not well within the economic structure of our country.

Many reasons are cited. One concerns the tax structure; another has to do with our international transactions. For some years now we have been placing more dollars in the hands of foreigners than they have either needed or were willing to spend for our goods and services—or to use, for that matter, to meet their commitments to us. This fact has had the natural result of the persistent deficit in our balance of payments. As the number of dollars in foreign hands* steadily increased, some of these foreign-held dollars were converted into gold. As a result, we saw our gold reserves significantly depleted. This accounts, in large measure, for the grave concern displayed in many banking centers abroad over the future stability of the dollar, as the backing of gold available in this country falls steadily lower. And while most foreign banking centers, for their own welfare, will aid us, this aid extended through international agreements will not be sufficient unless we ourselves take appropriate action. This was the situation which provoked the rather blunt talk on the part of European financial people to Secretary Dillon last fall. And many economists feel that our balance of payments problem will become even more acute in the future.

Thus how to meet this situation of such grave concern to us and to the other nations of the Free World is a matter requiring genuine priority in our strategic planning. Some of the Administration's most recent proposals are viewed by some as a barometer of sounder policies in the future. They would, for example, give the President increased authority to reduce our trade barriers in negotiating for reciprocal reductions by other nations. For a quarter of a century now, the United States has taken the lead in promoting freer international trade. In contradiction to this, how-

---

*Short term liquid liabilities as of May, 1962 were approximately 23.5 billion dollars.

ever, we also have a tax bill, sponsored by the Administration, which in effect proposes limitations upon the free movement of American private capital into foreign ventures—even though its purpose is to promote business and exports.

As contrasted with the Russian economy, state-controlled and directed, ours is a private, market-oriented system. It is sparked by the quest for profits and fueled by the flow of resources to provide the goods and services necessary to meet private demand through development of new products and sales expansion. It depends primarily on private decision-making in terms of purchases, production, savings, and investment—as well as on the continued expansion of productive facilities and other capital assets. Thus, when a businessman decides to invest in plant and equipment, purchase materials, hire workers and produce a product, he is governed by two major factors, the expectation of future sales and profits on the one hand, costs and the availability of resources on the other. If materials and labor costs seem too high in comparison to estimates of possible market prices, he is unlikely to consider the profit potential worthwhile. Also, he is concerned with profits after taxes—the ability to earn for his stockholders a satisfactory net return on invested capital. The investor who is his source of capital is similarly concerned. He is looking for returns upon his investment. He is naturally concerned with the ability of the proposed business venture to generate sufficient net earnings to compensate him adequately for the risk he takes.

Thus, we see a series of complex factors: the economy expands or fails to expand; jobs are created or unemployment rises; economic resources are efficiently utilized or they are not—and all these factors depend upon, and are influenced by, the thousands of complex, constantly changing decisions that are always being made throughout our economic system.

This is a far different situation than exists in the Soviet Union. There, the central government can determine as it sees fit the allocation of all resources to accomplish its national purposes. Naturally, in such a nation, the government's role in major policy formulation is entirely different than ours. The proper governmental role in our economy is for the President to set the priorities in the public sector of spending, while trying to encourage creativity and investment in the private sector, rather than trying to regiment it.

But there is little use in contrasting our economy with that of the Soviet Union, unless some among us have or have had intention of emulating that nation's policies. That American officials on occasion may succumb to the temptation of imitating aspects of Russian procedures is evidenced by the remarks of Seymour E. Harris, who is currently Senior Consultant to the Secretary of the Treasury.* Wrote Mr. Harris:

In some respects . . . the allocation of resources (in the Russian economy) commands approval: with the government determining the use of resources primarily, there is a tendency to put first things first—workers' housing before luxurious hotels; bread before cake; essential clothing before luxuries; education before travel.

Whether we intend imitation or not, however, we may still inadvertently impair our own economic system by adopting policies of restriction and control in the

---

*Saving American Capitalism, Knopf, 1950, p. 157.

private sector—by enlarging the role of government and by increasing government expenditures. What rationale could dictate these policies? Fear of the Soviet economy's supposedly superior rate of growth!

Colin Clark, the noted British economist quoted earlier, says that economic growth means "increasing the capacity to produce the goods and services required to provide improved living conditions." But this is a "measuring stick" applied differently in the Soviet Union than in our own country. The Soviet state-controlled economy regulates the rate of growth in *specific sections* of its economy, and in a direct manner. It can, for example, concentrate resources on capital formation in steel producing facilities, railroads, and other heavy industry, in the development of missiles and modern weapons, by starving other sectors of its economy— housing, consumer goods, and related areas. Many economists seriously question whether this procedure can materially increase the *over-all* rate of growth of the Soviet economy—particularly over any extended period of time. Mr. Clark asserts that Russia's "real rate of economic growth since 1953 has been lower than that of most industrial countries." Immediately after the war, he maintains, the years were marked by "universal shortage, when everything which could be produced was valuable; as production becomes more normal, marketing problems arise, even in Soviet Russia. 'Planned production' in fact turns out to be very wasteful, and does not achieve the high growth rates claimed for it."*

Such is Soviet growth. As to our own country, economic growth means an increase in the real national product as determined by the needs and desires of those

---

Growthmanship, op. cit.

who use and consume it. Production of goods which are
not needed or desired—in other words, goods which people won't buy—might increase the growth of national
product statistically, and from this it could appear that
the country was growing, but it would not be growth in
any meaningful sense. It is in this realistic distinction,
which we have and Soviets have not, that we see the
real meaning and true worth of our free market economy. It is impossible for our resources to be wasted in
the production of things that consumers do not want.
No private business can continue to operate unless its
products are saleable. The fabulous increase in our
levels of living over the years can be largely traced to
this fact.

Government-operated programs are on an entirely different footing. Not subject to the restraints and guides
that control industry, government programs often result
in waste. The Soviets face this problem constantly. The
British Government similarly, when the Labor Party
was in power during the post-war years, embarked on
various uneconomic schemes because of the lack of a
free market's restraints on waste. Meanwhile, in our
own country, we have been approximately doubling our
material standard of living every forty years. This continued increase in our real output of goods and services
is an attribute of our economy of which we can be justly
proud. Few, if any nations have had such a sustained
material growth continually passed on to the great body
of its citizens.

It can be seen, therefore, that government has an
important role to play in adopting policies which will
provide maximum aid and fullest flexibility for private
endeavor. While there are certain things that govern-

ment must do, and can do best, surely all reasonable people must agree that constant expansion of government expenditures (which alters command over resources) is not the way to attain maximum efficiency and growth in our economy! Rather, our government needs to look to the pursuit of policies which will stimulate the private sector, while avoiding the debilitating effects of stagnation or inflation. Although a nation never finds it easy to nudge a government back, principally because it is the government itself that must do the nudging,* there are ways in which government can limit itself to the role of accessory, stimulator, and creator of favorable settings, rather than to the role of an active participant on an equal footing with industry and business, a situation which may put industry and business at a disadvantage.

In any context, sound economic health in the private sector is essential. Nearly all observers, regardless of otherwise divergent views, agree that the American tax system has become a patchwork of inconsistencies and requires thorough overhauling. Tax reform strengthening the private sector would furnish increases in savings and aid the capital formation necessary to furnish jobs for our people, while at the same time creating the setting for a continuing rise in our material well-being. A recent book by Dr. Simon Kuznets, *Capital in the American Economy*, gives a lucid exposition of the necessity for long-range efforts to increase savings by altering our tax system in favor of individuals and corporations. As Dr. Kuznets points out, the United States relies more

---

*The human trait which makes it difficult for people in office to adopt measures curtailing their own power is one of the greatest dangers inherent in federal over-centralization. It is extremely difficult to reverse the process.

heavily upon a progressive income tax on individuals and businesses than any other major industrial nation. Furthermore, our tax treatment of allowances for depreciation and obsolescence of capital assets is far more stringent than that in other Western countries. The Common Market nations, for example, are much more liberal than we in allowing tax deductions for machinery and equipment. In order to help American business become more competitive with producers in other nations, to encourage savings and investment and the expansion of our industrial facilities, to provide full employment of our economic resources, including jobs for our growing labor force, and to continue the phenomenal increase in material well-being—to provide for all this plus an adequate national security, it is obviously necessary to give immediate attention to a substantial modification of our Federal tax structure.

The central factor in the tax structure is always the Federal budget. There are times in every nation's history when budget deficits become unavoidable and perhaps even necessary. But when an economy is operating close to full employment levels, massive government spending causing deficts is highly conducive to the type of inflation which, if continued year after year, can only lead to loss of confidence in our currency.

In addition to causing our steady inflation, the chronically "almost-balanced" and always growing federal budget directly saps our national strength. The continually expanding government command over economic resources drains away from other sections of our economy the capital which would otherwise be creating jobs and expanding industry. As Professor Paul McCracken, distinguished author and economist and member of the

Council of Economic Advisers in Washington from 1956 to 1959, points out: "We have made such an intellectual discipline and ritual out of economic growth that we may be in danger of leaving the key man and the key process out of the script—the entrepreneur and the process that we call innovation. We do not get growth by moving evenly in step on all industrial fronts—or spreading capital like successive layers of peanut butter all over the economy. Quite the contrary. We get it largely because of new products and new industries and new methods which succeed in making a successful assault on established markets and products and industries. . . . If we denigrate the status of the prime mover, the entrepreneur, and frown on letting the process destroy the old as well as create the new, we must not be surprised if the results are disappointing." We must face the fact that to have economic growth, some adverse effects will have to be borne, some industries will have to suffer, and some workers will have to find new employment. In Mr. McCracken's words: "Economic growth . . . has its harsh side. . . . Its path will certainly be strewn with the skeletons of industries and skills and jobs and professions whose replacement with something better is the essence of progress."

These are some of the reasons why I believe that we must carefully scrutinize every proposal for additional government spending—especially when such proposals carry the central government into areas formerly covered by private, or state and local government, activity. This returns us to the need for a sense of priorities in dealing with programs of government expenditure.

Legislation covering government spending is usually considered and passed individually, with little or no regard to what should be spent in the aggregate. Spending by priorities is a way to keep *within* the limits of growth in national income. In the past, national income has risen at the rate of three or four per cent each year, and projected estimates expect this increase to continue. If GNP were realistically estimated at $550 billion for fiscal 1963, and national income growth at about four percent, perhaps federal outlays should be increased by no more than $22 billion for 1964, and this $22 billion would serve as a ceiling. All proposed programs would then be considered according to the ceiling. Observance of the ceiling would be regarded as the general policy, and military and non-military spending for the cold war would have top priority, with no fixed ceiling being placed on them.

Subsumed under such a policy would be methods of implementation. It is obvious that, first of all, reform of the tax structure would be indispensable. The goal would be to design the tax structure so as to provide adequate revenue to cover the costs of the additional expenditures, and, when the economy is at reasonably full employment, provide moderate surpluses. Obviously, the $22 billion is merely an illustrative figure. To be realistic, it would have to be determined not for one year, but for five or even ten in order to preclude the necessity of having to adjust the tax structure upwards at too frequent intervals. In fact, the tax structure, under this proposal, should be overhauled *downward* at periodic intervals, lest revenues and outlays absorb too great a share of the growing national income. Mr. McCracken significantly points out that because our tax structure is progressive, "as incomes rise (into more highly taxed brackets), the ratio of total revenue receipts to national income will grow unless the tax structure is period-ically lowered." Assuming a continued national income growth of four per cent each year, with no change in the tax structure, federal revenues would increase by five or six per cent annually.

In summary, therefore, three reforms are necessary to construct an equitable and efficient tax structure: first, it should be redesigned to provide the revenues neces-sary to meet federal expenditures based on income growth, as well as to furnish a moderate surplus for emergency or unforeseen situations; second, it should be periodically lowered or overhauled so as not to absorb an ever larger proportion of the annual income growth and weaken the economic health of the nation; and, third, the progressive nature of the existing income structure should be closely scrutinized with a view to developing basic reforms able to remove the present inhibitions now preventing long-term growth and proper cyclical expansion.

Equally important is the determination of priorities. The priorities review committee, composed of experts appointed by the President to provide comparative anal-yses of inter-agency programs, would act as an adjunct to the National Security Council. If the government were thus able to determine, as outlined above, what amounts could reasonably be spent without jeopardiz-ing real growth or threatening inflationary spirals, a realistic guideline would be available for the Congress to distinguish urgent from less necessary legislation.

We possess adequate resources to win the cold war, if we but define our goals and priorities. Of course, we must spend whatever is needed to carry out a cold war policy of victory. No nation, however, can afford to squander its resources, especially when involved in such a protracted conflict. Even during actual shooting wars there should be recognition of the danger of waste. In the cold war there is equal need of this same recognition. It is time we understood the necessity of sacrificing some of the non-defense and non-essential legislative spending which we might be able to afford in a time of real peace.

Such a time of real peace is, of course, our goal.

11

A TIME OF TEST

IF THE WORLD OF THE WEST and its civilization dies in the struggle with Communism, it will not be so much an act of murder as one of suicide. The proper epitaph will not be that "they fought too hard," but that "they cared too little."

By all objective evidence there exists in the free world today the moral certitude, the physical power, and the cultural values required to roll back the barbed-wire frontiers of the Communist Empire, end its aggressions, and finally and fully keep the peace in a world of technological advances. If they were deflected from their present destructive orientation, the effects of the age-old enemies of hunger, poverty, disease, and ignorance could be lessened.

The crisis which now endangers us is not solely the fault of the present Chief Executive. It is also the fault of past indifferences and failures of understanding, in which most of us have participated or acquiesced. Mistakes made today merely reflect chaos created yesterday, and our task is to reconstruct those pillars of past policy that have proved themselves effective against chaos—the Marshall Plan, the Truman Doctrine, the Eisenhower-Dulles policy; and to construct unified strategic concepts

162

which, despite individual successes, we have lacked.

The test of Presidential leadership is the extent to which a President can rise above partisan politics and get on with the work at hand. This also is the test of Congressional responsibility, a test measured by the extent to which every legislator can stand aside from the press of day-to-day commitments—overwhelming though they may be—and come to grips with the crisis of our time, our freedom, our civilization, our basic values of liberty and integrity.

It seems to be a form of paralysis that is keeping us from measuring up to the tests, and is moving us instead toward the Western world's suicidal decline. The spiritual suicide of an individual occurs when regard for the opinions of others and the desire for personal popularity replace self-contained values as the motives of action. The suicide of a great nation can occur that way, too—by giving ultimate priority and heed to the opinions of others in a downward spiral chase for popularity. Already such a course has led to a national strategy which places mere biological survival on the same, or even a higher level than survival of our basic values, without which no proper public order can exist. These values are the freedom and dignity of the human personality, the rule of law, the acknowledgment of God beyond history and existence, and the moral order consequent to such an acknowledgment.

This course has led us to the weakness of seeking the popular approval of anxious bystanders, concerned merely with their own immediate self-interest, thereby causing us to renounce the strategy of initiative on which depends both their survival and our own. We have depended instead on a reactive and fragmented strategy, whose chief boast for almost a generation has been that *it may not offend the enemy!* It is notable, however, that John Foster Dulles cannot be included in this indictment. During his tenure as Secretary of State, many of his critics measured his effectiveness by the dubious yardstick of whether his policies met with popular approval, either here or abroad. Dulles' allegiance to his moral convictions, regardless of their popularity, was an example of the preference of statesmanship over political expediency.*

In contrast to the strategy which Dulles based on moral integrity, the boast of today's strategy is that it runs few risks. In reality, it runs all risks.

It flees like a lemming to drown in the waves of aggression that loom before it. It has led us, the most powerful nation in history, to forfeit historical leadership in the responsible use of power.

It has led us, in our foreign aid programs, to promote statism, with its inevitable curtailment of individual freedom. This it has also done in the name of concession to popular opinion.

It has led us, in our domestic economy, to leech away the potential of incentive to create jobs, promote real

---

*It was Dulles' attempt to formulate an overriding general strategy that first led me to explore the relative merits between reactive and fragmented foreign policies on the one hand, and a grand purposive strategy on the other. In my many conversations with this man, whom I greatly admired from the time of our first meeting, he repeatedly reaffirmed what was to him the cardinal requisite of foreign policy: that a nation to be an effective leader must be consistent, and that the consistency of that nation's actions must be based on something far more profound than a dedicated worship of statistics, isolated and considered as the sole factors for determining policy. That Dulles was not always successful, that even during his tenure our policies were sometimes fragmented and reactive can in great measure be attributed to the lack of an active, responsible, and rational public dialogue.

growth, and expand our economic strength. This, too, it has done to court popular opinion and to keep in step with discredited tunes piped by the opinions of other and even backward nations.

For all of this, we cannot blame the Communists. We alone bear the blame for all of these suicidal actions. Positivism, not Communism, is the philosophical virus that causes our paralysis, as Eric Voegelin has noted. It is positivism that paralyzes our efforts to formulate either an effective strategy of initiative or a coherent over-all policy.

Positivism, first defined by Auguste Comte, today permeates the entire Western World. It claims to be a scientific concept. It says that all we can know is what can be observed by the senses. It claims that what cannot be so verified cannot be *scientifically* known, and what cannot be scientifically known cannot be known at all. Thus, positivism elevates natural science to the altar as the standard of all knowledge, especially man's knowledge of himself and his social order. It dismisses the reality of man's spiritual experiences and becomes an ideology for a dehumanized clinic-world.

It is a profound lesson of history that as any nation increases its dedication to materialistic, positivistic criteria at the expense of dependence upon God and the truths beyond history, that nation has begun its downward course. Rome is the best-known example. Future historians may well view the Supreme Court's recent decision on religion in the schools as one such pivotal point in American history.*

Man yearns for a higher life, a truth beyond self. The

---

*In a 6-1 decision on June 25, 1962, the Court ruled that a non-denominational prayer recited daily in one of New York's public schools was unconstitutional.

anxiety of modern man, the anxiety facing Americans today, results from shallow positivistic philosophies which deny the truth that human nature seeks. As anxiety increases, we seek to satisfy it on the material level. We grasp at the utopian belief that science and government, bureaucratically directed, can somehow sweep in a materialistic heaven on earth, a final age where anxiety can no longer exist.

It is this which the former Chairman of the Political Science Department of Notre Dame, the Reverend Stanley Parry, has aptly called the civilizational crisis. It has been brought on by the shallow philosophy which seeks only expediency and adjustment, which believes only the physical senses, which forswears participation in the values that transcend mortal existence.

On the most dangerous level, positivism has even infiltrated religion, an infiltration which Dr. Karl Barth, the Swiss Protestant theologian, has exposed. Lecturing at the University of Chicago last spring, he took issue with the humanistic, introspective approach to religion in which man loses himself in behavorial self-examination. Barth said, "We must understand that the theme of the Church cannot be man's morals or feelings but God's encounter with man." Barth sees the Scriptures as an account of God's approach to man, not man's approach to God. In effect, Barth reacted against the humanist and empiricist approach to religion, which had left modern man in a maze, seeking in religion only another life adjustment process. These approaches rule out the validity of value judgments. Positivism disallows as sheer nonsense man's search for answers to the ultimate questions of his origin, his being and his destiny.

Positivism sees history developing through three

stages: the theological, the metaphysical, and finally the positive, or "highest stage" in history. Here of course there is an obvious parallel to Communist ideology, and its own final stage. The positivists define man's final progress as his emergence into pure materialism. This is presented as the victory of the mind's battle over "immaturity!" Part of this victory is that the "mature mind" supposedly ceases to inquire into the "good," and searches only for the "scientific." Obviously, this ideology gives priority to biological survival and physical existence. If it comes to a question of surrendering to the Kremlin or risking death, this ideology would dictate surrender. For death is the end, the destruction of everything, if only the material has reality or value. Following this ideology, the conviction of Plato that there is an essence beyond existence, is foolishness. The warning of Jesus, that we should not fear those who are able to kill the body, but those who are able to destroy the soul, becomes totally incomprehensible. And Patrick Henry, who cried "Give me liberty or give me death," must be regarded as having been insane.

The greatest stumbling block to the positivists is the fact that man not only has an instinct for evil, but he also possesses an instinct for good. Even the worst of men experience common love, common fear, common awe, common destiny. There is a quality of life that lifts us beyond ourselves. Every schoolboy who has played on a team knows what it means to play ball beyond his ability, for some inspired reason. This is not a phenomenon that can be observed in a test tube. It can be known only by participation. In the crude framework of positivism such facts must remain a mystery. Positivism cannot account for them in the world of sports. How much less, therefore, can positivism account for the countless larger versions of the same experience observable in every place on earth where man lives or dies for his beliefs?

Man, as has often been said, is incurably religious. As satisfaction for the religious craving, Comte cast out the worship of God to substitute the worship of humanity, and actually composed humanistic prayers—addressed to his mistress who figured in the liturgy as humanity's incarnate representative. Obviously such a worship can give way to all sorts of aberrant deifications, from the worship of Hitler to the worship of science, which is today's most tempting fashion in false deities. For science, even the same power of nuclear explosives that can destroy humanity, can also create miracles of accomplishment. Project Plowshare, our program of nuclear power for peaceful purposes, offers the hope of digging vast waterways, uncovering great oil reserves, blasting harbors, mass-producing diamonds, bringing water to deserts. Physicist Edward Teller sees the miracles of science as the answer to Malthus' pessimistic pronouncements on the population explosion, which he predicted would increase human needs beyond the world's capacity to supply them. At the same time, however, Teller notes the limitation faced—"our inability to get along with each other."*

Man cannot be controlled scientifically, as the positivists and empiricists would have us believe. He must act on real truths, and our policy for the survival of Western civilization must be based on reality. Yet, here is the difficulty—what do we mean by reality?

James Reston, close friend but sometime critic of

---

*See Edward Teller, *The Legacy of Hiroshima*, Doubleday, 1962.

President Kennedy, described on April 29, 1962, after the White House Correspondents Dinner, the "new Kennedy style in diplomacy." He called it, "the new reality, the decline in pretense and pomposity." Reston said, "it is a reflection of a serious effort by Kennedy to dispel some of the illusion of political life and deal with things as they are." For example, this new reality as interpreted by Reston was illustrated by President Kennedy's approach to Prime Minister Macmillan: "Tell me what you can and cannot do about joining Europe, and I'll do the same." Reston noted that this was precisely the attitude Kennedy also took to Vienna for his first encounter with Khrushchev. Reston said that the President was expressing in his own way Thoreau's love of reality. "Be it life or death, we crave only reality," said Thoreau. "If we are really dying, let us hear the rattle in our throats and feel cold in the extremities; if we are alive, let us go about our business."

But *is* this the final reality? In spite of Mr. Reston, I am convinced that Thoreau knew better. I am certainly not in favor of pomposity or pretense, but I feel that most of us have developed too much susceptibility to pragmatism; I would contend that our mere being alive and "going about our business" is not the final reality, and that when we are dying, the "rattle in our throats and the cold in our extremities" is also not the final reality. And, furthermore, there is no reality whatever in a bargain which one side enters in a spirit of deceit, intending to exploit the gullible good faith of the other. That this type of deceit is the classic Communist spirit cannot be doubted, and it obviously entered into the nature of any responses Khrushchev made to our young President's "new reality" as he approached the Communist dictator, with such charming informality, in Vienna. A short time later, it should be remembered, Khrush- chev began his vicious probe of the new President's quality by stirring up the ugly crisis in Berlin. Evident- ly, the "new reality" to some leaders looks suspiciously like mere softness.

In international bargaining of any kind, it is impera- tive to maintain an air of resolution—a credible resolu- tion, as well as resolution's internal spirit of firm deter- mination and coherent policy. This should be our aim even with our allies, Macmillan, de Gaulle, Adenauer, and others, for it is our responsibility as the world's most powerful nation to lead the way toward peace with jus- tice and freedom.

At the heart of the dialogue our country must face is the question long ago posed in Jerusalem—what is truth? This was the eternal query, phrased in his time by Pon- tius Pilate, and it lives on in the retort of the positivists who today ask what is reality? That prolific and agile writer, Arthur Schlesinger, Jr., Harvard historian and currently Special Assistant to the President, is one of the ablest articulators of the positivist point of view. He says, and I would agree, that an ideology "is not a pic- ture of actuality; it is a model, derived from actual- ity. . . ." Then he continues, "An ideology, in other words, is an abstraction from reality." That is where my agreement with Mr. Schlesinger would swiftly end. Mr. Schlesinger sees reality lying in the realm of empiricism, or what I have been calling positivism. He says: "The ideologist contends that the mysteries of history can be understood in terms of a clear-cut, absolute, central creed which explains the past and forecasts the future. Ideology thus presupposes a closed universe whose history is determined, whose principles are fixed, whose values and objectives are deducible from a central body of dogma. . . ." Then Schlesinger asserts the American liberal tradition has rejected this tradition, and now "sees the world as many, not as one." He notes William James, exponent of "pragmatism" and "radical empiricism," as having given the most brilliant expression of this philosophy, which animates today's liberalism.

It is precisely the empiricist philosophy which I believe has kept us from evolving a realistic dialogue in this country, and from formulating an effective over-all policy. It is the reason we are cast about on the turbulent sea of history and cannot discern the shore. Not that I disagree with every part of Mr. Schlesinger's statement. All of the ideologies—Communism, Fascism, Nazism, Socialism, Progressivism, and the one over which he and I most disagree, Positivism, are guilty of "historicism"—that is, of attributing every action of history to one factor or theory, whether economic determinism as in Communist dogma, or the "scientific approach" avowedly maintained by positivist philosophy. Basically, all these ideologies build a rigid system *within* history, *within* man's biological existence. This is why the word "historicism" is so apt.

But there is a reality *beyond* history, a reality to which history testifies, though Mr. Schlesinger persistently walls it off. His view of the world especially is confused by the multiplying crises of technology. Man has been able to smash the atom, but he has not been able to bring peace or freedom to the world. The reality beyond mere materialism can never be discovered by scientism, by test-tube observations. It can only be discovered by the daring of men willing to participate in events on a level of reality beyond existence, even though we can never fully possess that reality in this life. Only when America as a nation, and each of us as individuals, moves in this direction will we be able to say, as our Revolutionary forefathers did, "We hold these truths to be self-evident." Then our strategy will take on certainty; initiative will key-note our leadership; and the victory will not reside simply in the defeat of Communism, but in an order of true and general justice, freedom, and peace.

The civilizational crisis which positivism created has produced a spiritual vacuum which Communism has been filling. The hour is late. Today we can meet the peril. But tomorrow, unless we act now, the shadows will lengthen, and we may face the darkest age of mankind's history.

To man is given free will, and upon every American as upon our President rests the choice. The proposals of this book are those of one man, but I have heard long hours of testimony, both secret and unclassified, concerning matters of national security, I have listened to scholars and experts, and to ordinary citizens throughout grassroots America. The conclusions are mine, but what is represented in this book is a composite of much thought, and of the ideas of many people. Some conclusions are undoubtedly open to different interpretation. Almost certainly much has been overlooked, for the mass of material is too great for one small book. But every contribution is worth making if it contributes to realistic dialogue for a public strategy. On every level, presidential, congressional, state, or local, all should enter the dialogue.

I cited Eric Voegelin previously, and with him I will

close. In his analysis of history, he says that articulation is the condition of representative government. A society becomes "representative of itself," when it articulates itself, when it expresses itself deeply and fully, as, for example, in Lincoln's "government of the people, by the people, for the people." No constitution alone, and certainly no congress or parliament, can insure this type of representation. Conversely, Voegelin notes that our own foreign policy has been guilty of aggravating worldwide disorder by its naive efforts to superimpose representative institutions, when the conditions necessary for their function were not present.

Not since Lincoln's day of a house divided, has our nation faced such a crisis as now, when the whole world is divided, half-slave and half-free. The problem is not only the survival of our representative government through full articulation of all the people, but the crisis of an entire civilization, giving rise to the cold war with Communism on the one hand, and the breakup of Western values at home on the other hand. Our task would be far simpler if the real danger was the bomb, rather than the crises of men's beliefs, and whether they want more than mere biological survival. My hope is that in facing these issues, the people of this nation will begin to discuss with their leaders and with themselves, how we can form a strategy to meet this divided world. Just as we can achieve truly representative government only when all the people express themselves, so can we achieve public strategy for the victory of ordered freedom and the defeat of Communist slavery only when the people become articulate. To close off free expression or not to care, or to claim that we are really winning the cold war if we are not—these can build a gateway to the graveyard of our civilization. In schools and colleges, in the military, in the business and labor communities, among farmers, and in the household, these issues of Communism, positivism, and ordered freedom should be in the open—to be openly seen and openly discussed. For I would argue that we can never develop a strategy to meet the dilemma of our world, if that strategy is built upon the shifting sands of positivism and empiricism. These tend to give top priority to "survival only" in the hope that freedom and tyranny can marry and coexist.

For this hour, we were born. In the words of Washington, let us raise a standard to which all men may repair. And we might add with Lincoln, "We shall nobly save or meanly lose the last, best hope of earth."

12

EPILOGUE

HERE ARE THE SPECIFIC PRINCIPLES, in outline, that I would submit for consideration in the public dialogue we so desperately need to form a public strategy toward a world of peace with justice.

1. A public conviction that beyond biological existence is a quality of life, a moral order and a divine creation; that the risk of death in physical life is a secondary danger compared to the risk of death of these values and beliefs.

2. Morality, in this sense, is our willingness to place our ultimate concern beyond material values. Hence, the morality of the use of power is determined by whether it is used to promote order, stability, and a climate of freedom to find these values.

3. Within this and other nations, the type of orderly society we seek is one of limited government strong enough to meet its responsibilities and restrained enough to permit individual choice. According to the maturity of the nation and the wants of the people, this government may approach the representative form of a republic, a government of laws not of men. But a socialized democracy, where individuals have no real choice at the ballot box or in the market place, may have less

freedom than an England under Elizabeth the Great, or a France under General de Gaulle. On the one hand, statism breeds racial tensions and economic stagnation, and political corruption is greatest where we have one-party control. On the other hand, limitless freedom and abrupt revolution inevitably breed despots. The most perfect form of government ever devised was that of the checks and balances system provided under our Constitution, and it was the product of evolution, not revolution.

4. Formulation of our strategy and tactics cannot be relegated to computers, for inaccurate input will produce inaccurate output, and the Sino-Soviet strategists' use of deception makes inevitable the input of faulty information. The basic element of the Soviet strategy is the psychological offensive, employed to terrorize the West into the conditions for defeat. This is not a strategy that can be countered by machines: it must be met by minds possessed of clear and rational convictions.

5. While the Communists at present are emphasizing sublimited war, they might well move into a nuclear showdown if they ever achieve a breakthrough. We must not allow their "wars of colonial liberation" to distract us, therefore, from our own nuclear progress—from, for example, the military uses of outer space. There the decisive struggle may occur; and it is an area which the United States is at present neglecting.

6. We must accept the moral responsibility to use our power constructively to prevent Communism from destroying the heritage of our world civilization. In terms of military strategy, this means closing the strategy gap by a willingness to take the initiative in all areas. The President can properly orient the American people in

this strategy. Above all, while we have the power, we must aim at confronting the enemy directly. We can win every such confrontation.

7. There is no balance of terror, or lasting nuclear stalemate. Even nuclear deterrence can be upset by a Soviet breakthrough. At present we hold an overwhelming superiority, and we must translate it into political initiative *now*, for changing technological conditions and the possibility of Soviet breakthroughs could deny us this advantage in the future. We must rectify our current strategic mistake of a strategy subordinated to the Afro-Asian block in the United Nations, and rationally move to eradicate Communists from Cuba, protect Southeast Asia, and effect the unification of Germany.

8. Western build-up of forces for sublimited war is encouraging, but these tactics must be combined with a strategy of initiative which will eliminate Communism's use of privileged sanctuaries as a base of operation. We must develop methods capable of blunting Communist aggression, and we must be poised and ready with trained nationals from the captive nations to take advantage of another East German or Hungarian type of uprising.

9. The captive nations and the captive peoples of the Soviet Empire and Red China must be looked upon as allies who cannot be left to suffer permanently against their wills in a world half-slave and half-free. We must shun any agreement, in Berlin or elsewhere, which would appear to ratify the status quo and seal the doom of these peoples. We bear them a moral obligation.

10. Our foreign aid programs must be overhauled to give a primary role to the establishment of free, com-

petitive economies. We should give priority to our allies and to promoting those economies which allow their people choice in the market place. Promoting statism destroys the evolutionary process towards representative government, produces racial and class tensions, and confuses peoples as to what we stand for.

11. A stable, growing economy is essential to our sustained military effort in the cold war and our position of economic leadership in the world. A flight from the dollar will lead to an overwhelming Communist victory, equal economically to loss of United States leadership in the free world. The present profit squeeze will create increasing unemployment, jeopardize technological leadership, and hinder economic growth. A major overhaul of the tax system is mandatory; otherwise we shall face a serious collapse of the economy. It is essential to establish economic priorities to win the cold war, to give first priorities to the national security budget, and to spend on non-defense only amounts which will not injure the stability of the dollar. This is a sacrifice the American people must be willing to make.

12. The public must be encouraged to participate in a dialogue with each other, with their Congressmen, and with their President on winning the cold war. Only thus can a consensus develop, and only through debate on the ultimate concerns of our civilization can we find the pathway out of crisis.

13. The greatest threat to America is the lax thinking which sees all truths as relative and hence affords no reason for sacrifice in the cause of freedom. It is this attitude which has placed us on the defensive in the cold war. Uncommitted nations do not know where we stand, or for what we will fight. Humanity cannot reasonably

look for leadership from any nation or civilization that is uncertain of its values, uncertain even that there are values more important than physical survival.

Uncertain men may stay alive simply by sufferance of tyranny and sacrifice of soul. When they die, as all men must, they die in the terrible night of a humanity drained of nobility, stripped of justice and freedom. Such a night now is closing in on the world. We have the means to roll it back. We must—and we shall!